Perfect Phrases for Customer Service

D0029730

Also available from McGraw-Hill

Perfect Phrases for Performance Reviews by Douglas Max and Robert Bacal

Perfect Phrases for Performance Goals by Douglas Max and Robert Bacal

Perfect Solutions for Difficult Employee Situations by Sid Kemp

Perfect Phrases for Customer Service

Hundreds of Tools, Techniques, and Scripts for Handling Any Situation

Robert Bacal

McGraw-Hill

New York   Chicago   San Francisco   Lisbon
London   Madrid   Mexico City   Milan   New Delhi
San Juan   Seoul   Singapore   Sydney   Toronto

ISBN 0-07-144453-X

This is a *CWL Publishing Enterprises Book* produced for McGraw-Hill by CWL Publishing Enterprises, Inc., Madison, Wisconsin, www.cwlpub.com.

This publication is designed to provide accurate and authoritative informa-tion in regard to the subject matter covered. It is sold with the understanding that neither the author nor the publisher is engaged in rendering legal, accounting, or other professional services. If legal advice or other expert assis-tance is required, the services of a competent professional person should be sought.
    —*From a Declaration of Principles jointly adopted by a Committee of the American Bar Association and a Committee of Publishers*

McGraw-Hill books are available at special quantity discounts to use as premiums and sales promotions, or for use in corporate training programs. For more information, please write to the Director of Special Sales, Professional Publishing, McGraw-Hill, Two Penn Plaza, New York, NY 10121-2298. Or contact your local bookstore.

 This book is printed on recycled, acid-free paper containing a minimum of 50% recycled, de-inked fiber.

Contents

Contents

Contents

Part Two. Dealing with Specific Customer Situations   51

Contents

Contents

Contents

Preface

I want to share a little known secret about the value of delivering good service to customers. Yes, it's good for business and the organization. Yes, you may derive a lot of satisfaction by doing a customer service job well. No question. But what's the most compelling reason to learn about, and deliver good customer service? It's this. When you deliver good customer service to your customers, you experience less stress, and less hassle and grief from customers. They argue less. They're much less likely to insult, and they're less demanding. They don't threaten you when they get upset (I'll have your job!").

You can save huge amounts of time. One dissatisfied customer may take up to ten or twenty times more of your time than a satisfied one. And the time spent with the dissatisfied customer is usually not all that much fun. Customer service skills help you keep your happy customers happy, help prevent customers from becoming unhappy and taking out their frustrations on you, and help you deal effectively and quickly with customers who are upset and unhappy.

Preface

This book gives you the tools to interact with customers more effectively, so that the company, the customer, and you, the person dealing with the customer, all benefit. It's a different kind of book about customer service. It's not full of principles or platitudes, or handy customer service slogans. It focuses on *doing*. What should you *do* with a customer who is swearing at you? What do you *do* to prevent customers who have waited a long time from getting really angry? What do you *do* to provide advice to customers so it will be heard and appreciated? This book will answer these questions, and many other ones about customer service situations—specifically and precisely. This book is about *solutions*.

Organization

Part One of this book has two chapters. In Chapter 1, we'll cover some basics of customer service, so you can increase your understanding of what customers want from you, and the things that cause customers to hit the roof. We'll also talk about various types of customers (internal, external, paying and non-paying), and we'll explain how you can best use this book.

Chapter 2 describes dozens of very specific customer service techniques. The explanations will help you decide when to use what techniques and in what customer situations. The pages in that part of the book are shaded black so you can easily refer to them for specific techniques, which are given in alphabetical order.

Part Two, and the most important, covers 60 common and not-so-common customer service situations and tells you specifically how you can deal with them. I do this by

- describing the situation
- listing the techniques to use in this situation

- presenting a dialogue to show you exactly what to say and do
- explaining the reasoning behind the use of the techniques
- providing a few hints and tips to help you use the techniques properly

Even if we have not included all of the situations you deal with on the job, you will be able to extrapolate the examples to other situations you do face. I think that regardless of whether you work in retail, the hospitality industry, government, or as a call-in customer service rep, the situations covered in this part will be very useful to you.

Conclusion

Far too much customer service training and far too many customer service books tell you only what you already know. Do you really need to be told *again* that you should smile? Or shake hands? No. But you might find it useful to know when it's a *bad* idea to smile at a customer. You'll learn that from this book.

So, here's the bottom line about this book: you may come across a few things you already know. But you'll also come across a number of techniques you probably haven't thought about. If you work at using these techniques properly, and focus on *doing* things differently with customers, you are going to be better at your job, be clearly better at customer service than others who don't understand these techniques, and help your employer and yourself be more successful. And along the way, save yourself a lot of hassle and a lot of grief.

The Customer Service Zone Web Site

I've created a Web site called the *Customer Service Zone*, where you will be able to find hundreds of articles on customer service. Use of the site is free of charge. We have great plans for the site, including using it to add more customer service techniques, and more customer service dialogues you can learn from. We may even have a forum where you can ask questions and share your customer service expertise. To visit, go to **www.customerservicezone.com**. By visiting, you can continue to learn and develop your customer service skills.

Acknowledgments

I continue to be grateful to McGraw-Hill for providing the opportunity for my books to exist. Specifically, I'd like to thank Mary Glenn for her help in defining the focus of this book.

As usual, John Woods and Bob Magnan of CWL Publishing Enterprises have helped make this book what it is. Bob has edited all my books, and as always has carried out his job on this one with great patience and skill.

Finally, my wife, Nancy has to put up with all the angst and craziness from me that always accompanies a book project. Thank you for taking on additional responsibilities so I could concentrate on getting this book done.

About the Author

Since the early 1990s Robert Bacal has trained thousands of people in how to deal with difficult customers through his "Defusing Hostile Customers" seminar. His clients have included people from a wide range of specializations, ranging from health care, law enforcement and security, social work, education, and manufacturing.

He draws from a range of disciplines, including psychology and psycholinguistics, and has incorporated a number of customer service techniques that have come from some of the attendees at his seminars. He holds a masters degree in psychology from the University of Toronto, and a B.A. from Concordia University in Montreal.

He is the author of the *Defusing Hostile Customers Workbook For Public Sector* and a similar book written for school board officials, teachers, and educators. He is also author of two titles in McGraw-Hill's Briefcase Books series, *Performance Management* and *Manager's Guide to Performance Reviews* as well as *The Complete Idiot's Guide to Consulting* and *The Complete Idiot's Guide to Dealing with Difficult Employees.*

He makes his home near Ottawa, Canada, where he continues to write, and offer customer service related seminars. He also hosts The Customer Service Zone on the Internet, at **www.customerservicezone.com**, where you can find free help and suggestions on customer service improvement.

Part One

Succeeding at Customer Service

Chapter 1
Basics of Customer Service

There must be a billion words written about customer service. Advice abounds, from the banal and obvious (smile when you talk on the phone) to complex and difficult suggestions about how to "create a corporate culture of excellent customer service."

Amidst all of the words, simple or fancy, is hidden a basic truth about customer service: the person who interacts directly with the customer determines whether that customer perceives that he or she is receiving poor customer service, excellent service, or something in between. If you serve customers directly, *you* have the power to affect their perceptions. That customer contact is where "the rubber meets the road."

If you provide service to customers, your words and behaviors are the tools you use to create a positive customer perception of you and the company you work for. Whether you are a novice working with customers or a seasoned pro, what you do and say will affect how customers see you. You can't help it. Customers will form opinions, so you might as well learn how to create positive opinions. But you need to know how to do that.

3

That's what this book is for—to teach you about the dozens and dozens of techniques you can use when interacting with customers so they will walk away with positive feelings about the experience. You'll learn about very specific things you can do or say in all kinds of customer interactions. You'll learn how to deal with difficult customers. You'll learn how to approach customers and how to get information from them so you can do your job. You'll learn to deal with customer service problems quickly, efficiently, and professionally. Best of all, the techniques in this book will fit your needs, whether you serve burgers, staff the desk in a hotel, help people in health care environments, or even work in government.

This book will tell you exactly what to do and say and it will provide you with numerous examples so you can use customer service techniques effectively.

Let's get started!

What's in It for Me?

Why should you be concerned with providing excellent customer service? You don't own the company. You may not get paid more for providing excellent customer service. So, what's in it for you?

There are three powerful reasons for learning to provide great customer service: greater job satisfaction, reduced stress and hassle, and enhanced job success.

First, very few people can derive any job satisfaction when they feel that the time they spend at work is "wasted." Most of us need to feel useful and productive—to make a difference, whether it's helping a fast food customer make healthier food choices or dispensing legal advice. When you provide high-quality customer service, you feel that you are making that difference and can derive pride in your work.

When you do a good job with a customer, such as calming down someone who is angry and complaining, you feel good about having achieved something. But perhaps more important than your own perceptions is the customer's perceptions, when you do a good job with a customer and he or she tells you what you have achieved. That feedback really helps you feel good about yourself and the job you're doing. Doing a good job and taking pride in your customer service accomplishments is a way to prevent job burnout.

Second, learning to deliver quality customer service will save you a lot of stress and hassle. When you learn and use customer service skills, you are far less likely to get into protracted, unpleasant, and upsetting interactions with a customer. You make yourself less of a target for customer wrath. That's because customer service skills help keep customers from becoming angry and help reduce the length and intensity of the anger when and if difficult customer service situations occur.

Third, learning and using quality customer service techniques helps form the perceptions of those who may be able to help your career—supervisors, managers, and even potential employers. Using them makes you look good to everyone: that's critical in getting promoted, receiving pay raises, and getting new job opportunities. Managers and supervisors tend to notice when customers ask for you specifically because you do such a good job or contact them to provide positive comments about how you've helped.

Of course, you may have other reasons to want to provide the best customer service possible. You may want to contribute to the success of your employer. You may like the feeling of having other employees look up to you as a good model. Or you may even benefit directly if you work on a commission basis; people who are good at customer service do earn more.

Regardless of your reasons, you can learn how to use quality customer service techniques and serve your customers better.

In the rest of this chapter, we'll provide an overview of customer service principles and issues and explain how to use this book. In the next chapter, we'll describe 60 techniques you should be using. The rest of the book is dedicated to showing you how to use those techniques.

Different Kinds of Customers

Before we continue, we should clarify what the word "customer" means.

You are probably familiar with our starting definition: *the customer is the person who pays for goods or services that you provide.* This definition works in some contexts, but not all. It breaks down in situations where money does not directly change hands. For example, people often interact with government, public schools, and other organizations: they receive goods or services from them, but do not pay anything directly to them. We need to change our definition so that people who interact with these organizations fall under our definition of customer, since they, too, deserve high-quality customer service, even if they are not paying directly.

Here's a better definition: *the customer is the person next in line who receives your output (service, products).* That person may purchase goods or services directly or receive output you create or deliver without direct payment. The person may be outside your company, but this definition also includes anyone within the company who receives output from you.

Let's be more specific. There are four basic types of customer. Regardless of type, each customer deserves to receive top-quality customer service. Also, regardless of the type of customer, you and your organization will benefit by providing top-quality customer service.

First, there are *external paying customers*. These are the people who pay to eat in a restaurant, pay for health care and legal advice, or pay to stay in a hotel.

Second, there are *internal customers*. These are people who receive output (services, products, information) that you create or provide, but who are in the same organization. Internal customers may sometimes be billed via interdepartmental charge systems or there may be no payment system in place. For example, human resources staff involved in hiring employees are, in effect, working on behalf of internal customers (the managers of the work units needing new employees). The technician who maintains company computers is working for internal customers (the people who use the computers he or she maintains).

Third, there are *external nonpaying customers*. These customers receive services, goods, or other outputs but do not pay directly for them. For example, the tourist who visits a traveler's information kiosk by the highway may receive tourist information (outputs) and maps (goods), but is not paying directly. That tourist is a customer. Another example is the parent who attends the parent-teacher meeting at the local public school: he or she receives outputs and services from the teacher, but does not pay the teacher directly. That parent needs to be treated like a customer, too.

That brings us to the fourth type of customer, *regulated customers*. Government organizations often interact with people in ways that are not oriented toward providing something to individuals, but are instead toward regulating them for the common good. It might seem like people regulated by the government through licenses, zoning regulations, permits, and other controls are really not customers. But we want to include them, because even though government is regulating them, they still deserve the best possible levels of customer service. Including this group under the term "customer" reminds us (and, hopefully, government employees) that even when employees are telling people what to do or what they are allowed to do, they need to do so applying principles of customer service.

First Things First—Dispelling an Important Customer Service Myth

We need to address the single most popular false idea about customer service. No doubt you've heard the phrase, "The customer is always right." It's a great slogan, credited to H. Gordon Selfridge, who passed away in 1947. Unfortunately, it's wrong and misleading.

Clearly the customer is not always right. Customers make unreasonable requests and sometimes have unreasonable expectations. Sometimes customers play fast and loose with the truth. Customers may not understand your company and what you can and can't do for them.

Practically speaking, you can't operate under the assumption that the customer is always right. You can't give each customer what he or she asks for.

So, can we come up with a phrase or two that realistically

describe how we should treat customers? Yes. Here are two short phrases that fit the bill.

- The customer always deserves to be treated as if he or she is important and his or her opinions, needs, and wants are worthy of listening to.
- The customer deserves to receive maximum effort on the part of those serving him or her, even when the customer's expectations, wants, and needs may be impractical.

Since the customer isn't "always right" and it's often not possible to give the customer what he or she wants, what are the implications for customer service?

It's simple. Customers have other important wants and needs. Even in situations where you can't do what the customer asks, you *can* contribute to the customer's development of a positive impression about *how* he or she is treated. That's what we've captured in the two phrases above. We need to focus not only on *what* we provide to the customer, but on *how* we provide it. That's the key to realistic excellent customer service. To do that, you need to understand these other wants and needs—and that's where we are going to go next.

Understanding What Customers Want

One thing about the customer service techniques you are going to learn: you can't succeed with them by memorizing them or using them in every situation. The key to customer service is doing the right thing at the right time.

To be able to choose the right techniques and to use them effectively, you have to understand what customers want. Knowing this will help you make sense of the techniques you'll be looking at. Below is a list of the most important customer wants and needs. When you address these, you create positive customer perceptions about you and your company, which means fewer arguments, fewer hassles, and better customer relationships.

- problem solved
- effort
- acknowledgment and understanding
- choices and options
- positive surprises
- consistency, reliability, and predictability
- value (not necessarily best price)
- reasonable simplicity
- speed
- confidentiality
- sense of importance

Customers want their *problem solved*. They want to get what they want from you, whether it's a product, service, or other output. This is the customer service "want" that most people are familiar with. However, it's not always possible to give the customer what he or she wants, which is where the rest of the "wants" come in. Even if you can't solve the customer's problem, you can create positive perceptions by addressing the other, less obvious customer wants.

Customers expect that you (and your company) will *make an effort* to address their problems, concerns, and needs, even if you can't give them what they want. Customers respect effort, often pay attention to effort above and beyond the call of duty, and will turn on you (create hassles) if they sense that you are not making an effort. Many of the techniques you will learn later in this book work because they demonstrate "effort above and beyond the call of duty."

Customers want and expect to have their wants, needs, expectations, feelings, and words *acknowledged and understood.* That means listening and proving to the customer that you have "got" what he or she is saying. Customers who feel understood and acknowledged feel important: that's a vital part of good customer relationships.

Customers also want to feel they have *choices and options* and are not trapped by you or your company. They want to feel they are making the decisions and that you are helping them, rather than the other way around. When customers feel helpless or powerless, they tend to more likely become frustrated, angry, and aggressive.

Customers also appreciate *"positive surprises."* Positive surprises are things you may do that go above and beyond their hopes and expectations (going the extra *five* miles). They include offering discounts or providing some other benefit that is normally not available to them. Positive surprises are most useful when dealing with difficult or angry customers.

Consistency, reliability, and predictability are also important customer wants. Customers expect that you will treat them in a consistent way and that you will do what you say you will do each and every time. By acting in accordance with these wants, you provide the customer with a sense of security and confidence in you personally and in the company. This builds loyalty.

Customers also expect *value* for their investments of time and money. What's interesting here is that while money (price) is part of the value equation, it is only a part. When customers look at value, they also take into account how they are treated, the quality and expertise of the advice they receive from you to help them make decisions, and a number of other factors. You may not be able to affect the price of services or products you provide, but you can add value by helping the customer in other ways.

Reasonable simplicity is also an important customer want. These days many people are overwhelmed by a complex world. If you complicate the customers' world or make them jump through a number of hoops, they will become frustrated and angry. One of the your customer service roles should be to make things easier for the customer, not more complicated, without oversimplifying or treating the customers in a condescending way.

Speed and prompt service are also important wants on the part of customers. At minimum, they want you to make the effort to help them quickly and efficiently. They also expect that you will not create situations that have them waiting around unnecessarily. While you may not always be able to control how fast a customer is served, you can convey a sense that you are working at top speed.

Confidentiality is an important aspect of customer service. Clearly customers want you to keep their sensitive information to yourself, but it goes further than that. Customers may also want some degree of privacy even when talking to you about what may seem to be a mundane or nonsensitive issue. Customers may feel uncomfortable if there are other staff or other customers crowding around them.

We've left the most important need for last. Customers need the sense that *they are important*. Many of the above wants tie into this. Listening to and acknowledging customers demonstrates that you believe they are important. So does arranging for pleasant surprises or making an effort. Many of the specific phrases and techniques you are going to learn tie directly into helping the customer feel important.

About This Book

There is no "right" way to use this book, so you'll need to find what works for you. We end this chapter by explaining the format of the book, providing some suggestions about how to get the most out of it, and discussing how this book can be used to help others learn the customer service skills described in it.

Format

This book is broken into three parts. The first consists of this chapter, which provides an overview of some essential aspects of customer service. The second part provides brief summaries of the specific and practical customer service skills you will be learning.

The third part is the real heart of the book. In the third part, you will see customer service skills in action and in context. We will describe a particular customer service situation and indicate which techniques are being demonstrated in the example. You will then see a brief dialogue that describes what the customer says and does and how the employee in the example deals with the situation by applying the specific customer service skills. After each dialogue you will find an explanation that will help you understand why the employee chose to use these specific techniques and how they work.

We will also provide hints and tips and cross-reference to other dialogues that may relate to the particular example.

How to Get the Most from This Book

Some people will prefer to read the book from cover to cover, which can be effective. We suggest that you read the first and second parts carefully before you move on to the specific dialogues and examples, since doing so will help you make sense of the specific applications of the techniques.

However, you may prefer to browse or to look for specific solutions to specific customer service situations that are particularly relevant to you. That's fine, too.

If you would like to be systematic and organized about learning customer service techniques, you might want to cover one example a day. Each day you can spend five minutes on a particular example, then try to use the techniques in your work. You can learn in small bits, which keeps you from being overwhelmed.

Hints

We have tried to include dialogues and examples from many professions and job types. The specific techniques for customer service are universal and apply across almost all customer situations. Even if the examples do not pertain directly to the kind of work you do, you'll learn how the techniques in the examples can and should be used. So, don't be put off if the example isn't quite perfect for your job. Adapt it as necessary.

When you are looking at the techniques and examples, keep in mind the links to the customer wants described in this chapter. Think about how the techniques can be used to help the customer understand that you believe he or she is important and that you are making an effort. That will help you understand the proper use of the techniques.

For Those Wanting to Help Others Learn Customer Service Skills

Managers, supervisors, and trainers may want to use this book as a basis for training others in customer service skills. The design of this book makes it easy to do so, since it's short, concise, and modular. Learners need not be exposed to the entire book at one time or in one training session; individual skills can be covered quickly, even in short lunch time meetings or staff meetings.

We are planning to produce a free, short guide for those who want to use this book to train others in the skills discussed here. At this time, we don't have a release date. It will be made available in electronic form from our customer service support site at www.customerservicezone.com. Even those not considering training others may want to visit this free site, since it contains numerous resources you may find useful in enhancing your own customer service skills.

Time to look at the tools of customer service—the things you can do and say to deal effectively with customer service situations that run from the basic and simple to the very challenging and difficult.

Chapter 2
Customer Service Tools and Techniques

There are tools and techniques for every trade and profession. Carpenters have their hammers, saws, screwdrivers, and scores of other tools and techniques for using them. Plumbers have their pipe wrenches and pipe cutters and benders and the rest. Other professionals—accountants, doctors, psychologists, and so on—also have tools and techniques. Those involved in customer service are no different, although they use less tangible tools than carpenters and plumbers. The tools and techniques of effective customer service have to do with what employees say and do with reference to each customer.

Top-notch customer service employees know how to use each specific tool and how to match tools to specific situations. When you understand the tools available and understand the basics of customer service from the introduction, you'll be able to choose the *right* tools for each customer service "job."

In this section, we are going to describe and explain each of the major customer service tools at your disposal. Since customer service involves human interactions that are not always predictable, using these tools cannot always guarantee the positive result we might want. However, using these tools increases the chances of a successful interaction with each customer, whether that customer is currently happy or is angry and upset.

Since Part Two contains numerous examples of how to use the customer service techniques and tools, the descriptions in this section will be relatively short. You will find that in real life it won't always be easy to determine whether a "perfect phrase" is part of one customer strategy or another. That's because some phrases can actually fit more than one response and because some of the strategies overlap. Don't worry about what a strategy is called. Try to understand how the strategy might work and how you might use it or modify it to improve customer service.

Strategies are presented in alphabetical order.

Customer Service Tools and Techniques

Above and Beyond the Call of Duty

Going above and beyond the call of duty means doing something that is not required of you as part of your job or obligations to your customer. It means doing something special or extra. Customers, even difficult ones, often display extreme gratitude and loyalty when you can show them that they are so important that they are worth going beyond what is required. And that's one of the secrets to good customer service—demonstrating through your actions that your customer is important and special.

Acknowledge Customer's Needs

When a customer sees that you are making an effort to understand his or her needs (even if you can't meet them), it is more likely the customer will view you positively. Acknowledging needs may involve rephrasing something the customer has said to you (e.g., "I understand that you want to get the best value for your money") or it may involve responding to something you observe about the customer (e.g., "I can see that you must be in a hurry").

Acknowledging Without Encouraging

When you deal with an angry or difficult customer, it's important to prove to him or her that you understand the facts surrounding the situation that is upsetting and the feelings the customer is experiencing. The catch is that "what you focus on, you get more of"—and you don't want to encourage the customer to continue being difficult or continue angry behavior that interferes with helping the customer. Acknowledging Without Encouraging really involves the combination of two techniques.

The first set involves using both empathy statements and refocus statements together. First, you acknowledge the feelings in a short sentence and, without stopping, you refocus or steer the conversation back to the problem and away from the customer's emotions.

Similarly, you can do the same thing around demonstrating your understanding of the facts of the customer's situation by combining active listening with refocusing. Reflect back your understanding of the customer's situation and then refocus back to problem solving.

The important thing to remember is the principle. You need to acknowledge the facts of the situation and the emotions, but you don't want to dwell on them. Focusing on them results in longer interactions that tend to be more emotional.

Active Listening

Active listening proves to the customer that you are paying attention and that you believe that the customer and what he or she has to say are important. Active listening involves rephrasing the key points of what the customer has said and reflecting them back to the customer, often in the form of a question. For example: "So, you're saying that you're sure there are parts missing from the product and you want a complete refund. Is that right?"

Admitting Mistakes

People in general and, of course, customers in particular tend to respect those who are honest and open about mistakes and errors and who take responsibility rather than avoiding it. When mistakes occur, it is often good strategy to admit to the mistake, whether you made it personally or the company you represent made it. Even if you are not completely sure where the problem occurred and who made a mistake, it's possible to admit the *possibility* of a mistake. This avoids unnecessarily provoking a customer by representing yourself or the company as infallible.

The key thing in admitting mistakes is to do so in a very short sentence and then move on to *solving* whatever problem exists.

Allowing Venting

You are probably familiar with the concept of venting. By allowing the customer to let off steam uninterrupted, the idea is that the customer will eventually calm down on his or her own. While this may work, you should know there are two types of people. Venters are people who will calm down if allowed to let off steam. Obsessors, however, will get angrier and angrier the more they talk about their upset or grievances.

If you allow a person to vent, and find s/he is getting more and more agitated, more active measures are needed, such as empathy statements, attempts to refocus, neutral mode and so on.

Apologize

A *sincere* apology can help calm a customer, particularly when you or your company has made an error. You can apologize on behalf of your company. Keep in mind that tendering an apology does not necessarily mean that you are admitting culpability. As with admitting a mistake, your apology should be "short and sweet," followed by refocusing on solving the problem or addressing the customer's needs.

Perfunctory or insincere apologies are worse than saying nothing and anger customers. Also, due to a general overuse of the words "I'm sorry," apologies are not as powerful as you might think. They should always be used along with other techniques.

Appropriate Nonverbals

Nonverbals are body language. Customers tend to decide whether you are interested in them and want to help them based on whether you look at them when you speak (or listen), whether you stand or sit in an attentive posture, and even if you fidget or look like you are in a hurry to get rid of them.

Appropriate Smiles

Most customer service training stresses the importance of smiling. There's no question that a warm smile is valuable. However, and it's a big "however," smiles (and other facial expressions) must fit the situation. For example, if a customer is exceedingly upset about how she has been treated, smiling at the customer might be seen as smirking, adding fuel to the fire. That's why smiles need to be appropriate to the situation and the customer's state of mind. Smiling at the wrong time can send the message that you aren't taking the customer seriously.

Arranging Follow-Up

Not all customer problems can be addressed immediately. Many situations call for some form of follow-up or additional communication. For example, if you don't have an answer to a customer's question, you might arrange to find out and call the customer back within a few minutes. Proper follow-up tells the customer he or she is important to you.

Arranging follow-up should include three things: explaining what you will do between now and the actual follow-up, giving a specific time by which you will get back to the customer; and offering a choice as to the form and timing of the follow-up (e.g., you call back, you send an e-mail, the customer calls you). Needless to say, when you arrange a follow-up, you *must* be able to fulfill your promise—and you must do so.

Assurances of Effort

When customers don't feel you are making an effort, they get angry. On the flip side, when customers feel you are making an effort above and beyond the call of duty, they are less likely to target you for angry behavior if they can't get what they want.

An assurance of effort is a statement that tells the customer you will do your best to meet *his or her* needs. For example: "I can see you are in a hurry and I'm going to do my best to get this wrapped up in a few minutes."

Notice that an assurance of effort is different from an assurance of results. You can always assure the customer that you will try, even if you do not yet know if you can give the customer what he or she wants.

Assurances of Results

An assurance of results is a stronger statement than an assurance of effort: it promises that the customer will have his or her problem resolved. An assurance of effort doesn't promise results, so it can be used in almost any situation. Assurances of results should be made only when you can legitimately guarantee the results you are promising.

Audience Removal

Some angry customers will "play to the audience" in public situations where others are present. You can tell whether this is happening by observing whether the customer seems to be looking to other customers or other bystanders for approval or to be addressing them. Removing the audience involves arranging for the customer to be served away from the audience, usually in an office space or somewhere away from the audience. Here's an example of how to do it: "Mr. Jones, I'm sure you'd prefer that your privacy is protected, so let's go to the office and we can continue there."

Bonus Buyoff

This technique involves offering something of value to the customer as compensation for inconvenience or other problems. The offer need not be of significant monetary value, since the point is to be perceived as making an effort. It is used primarily when the organization has made an error, but it can also be used when an error has not been made and the employee wants to make a goodwill gesture.

Broken Record

This technique is used primarily with customers who won't work with you to solve their problems. Its intent is to send the message: We're not going to continue the conversation until we deal with the specific issue that I want to deal with.

It involves repeating the same message, but in different words, until the customer starts to work with you. For example: "You have several options. [Describe them.] Which would you prefer?"

If the customer ignores this, you repeat the message, but in different words: "You can [option one] or [option two]. Do you have a preference?"

The same message can be broken recorded four or five times, until the customer finally chooses one.

It can also be used for expressing empathy, with a customer who is too angry to engage in specific problem solving.

Closing Interactions Positively

A relatively simple technique to end conversations, closing interactions positively usually involves offering pleasantries (e.g., "Thanks for coming in" or "I appreciate your patience and apologize for the delay"). You want to end each interaction, even if it's difficult, on a positive note.

Common Courtesy

Common courtesy refers to a number of behaviors that are based on consideration and polite behavior standards in your country or area. They're basic and you probably know what they are, but it's important not to lose sight of the importance of using "please" and "thank you," creating an environment for your customer/guest that is inviting, and using civil language. You can add your own ideas to what constitutes common courtesy for the people you serve.

Even with such simple techniques, there are one or two important points to keep in mind. When employees involved in customer service are under stress or rushed, they tend to stop using common courtesy. It's a natural mistake. In trying to address the customer's needs quickly (being task oriented), it's easy to forget that the process (how you interact with the customer) is important. You need to use common courtesy even when you are rushing to meet the needs of your customer, unless it's an emergency situation (e.g., a health emergency) where common courtesy may delay critical actions (e.g., calling 911 for expert help).

Also, remember that when you most need to use common courtesy is in the situations where you least feel like it. Difficult and obnoxious customers tend to push employees to respond rudely or at least curtly. Unfortunately, when you neglect common courtesy, problems escalate, so it's in your interests to be polite and courteous, even with the people you feel don't deserve it. It isn't about who deserves common courtesy, but what will work and reduce the time you waste.

Completing Follow-Up

Obviously, when you have arranged for follow-up, you need to complete the follow-up. There may also be situations where a colleague or your boss asks you to follow up on something. It's a simple process. Contact the individual. Identify yourself. Explain *why* you are following up. Request any information you need. Respond to the customer's problem/issue as needed.

Contact Security/Authorities/Management

Most employees are not trained in security, self-defense, or other methods for dealing with a violent, highly disruptive, or potentially violent customer. If it's not your job, it's not your job. Don't take on the responsibilities of security or the police. When you are faced with any situation that may be violent or pose a security threat, contact security personnel, management, and/or the police. If your company has a policy on this issue, follow it. Do not chase customers or attempt to apprehend them. This strategy also applies in situations where someone has made some sort of threat to you personally or to the company. At minimum, notify your manager immediately. Remember that safety is your first priority—for yourself, your colleagues, and other customers.

Disengaging

Disengaging is a technique that is most often used with a difficult or aggressive customer. It has several purposes: it serves to temporarily halt a conversation that is getting increasingly emotional and unpleasant and it is used if a conversation is going around in circles.

Disengaging means taking a break from the interaction to allow both parties to calm down or think more clearly so that, when the conversation resumes, it's more like a "fresh start." When you are in a situation in which the conversation is not likely to result in success, it's possible to offer a reason to stop and resume in a minute or two or after an even longer interlude. For example, you might say, "Mr. Smith, let me take a minute to check your file," and then suspend the conversation while you go check. You can also take the more direct approach, as follows: "Mr. Smith, maybe we both need a break so we can approach this fresh. How about if we resume this discussion tomorrow? We can set up a time that's convenient." This technique can be used in person and on the phone.

Disengaging is similar to using a time-out. A time-out is used to allow the customer to calm down by giving him or her an opportunity alone. Disengaging does not require the customer to be alone, but relies on the suspension of the conversation for its power.

Distraction

This technique is used with angry customers to shift their attention away from their anger and away from expressing their anger at you. It's designed to break the anger cycle. It works like this: direct the customer's attention to a physical object with words and with a gesture, so the customer needs to break eye contact with you. Here's an example: "If you'll take a look at the computer screen [swivel monitor and point to a specific spot on the monitor], you'll see that we have your policy expiry date as November 6. That's where the problem is."

Any physical object—brochures, forms, signs—can be used, but the object should have some relevance to the issue being discussed.

Empathy Statements

Empathy statements are used as primary responses to any situation where the customer is upset or frustrated or even might become frustrated or angry in the future. They are intended to prove to the customer that you understand his or her emotional state or why he or she is feeling that way. You need not agree with the reason why a customer is angry, but you need to acknowledge that the customer is angry. Here are some examples:

- "It seems like you are pretty upset by the delay."
- "I know it can be frustrating to have to complete these forms."

■ "You must have been pretty upset to find out the product didn't work."

Here's the key to effective empathy statements. Be specific. Name the emotion (anger, frustration, upset) and identify the source of the emotion (the delay, the forms, the product failure). Avoid general statements like "I see where you are coming from."

Expediting

Expediting means "making things go faster." In other words, give the impression that you are doing things to speed up whatever process the customer is trying to get done. You can convey this by talking more quickly and more emphatically, while clearing away barriers that may be slowing down progress toward getting what the customer wants.

Expert Recommendations

Customers don't always know what they want or need or they may be confused about what to do next. One of the roles of someone in customer service involves providing expert advice or recommendation about product selection or about the most efficient way for the customer to accomplish what he or she wants. Before giving advice or recommendation, it's always good to ask the customer if he or she would like you to provide it. Here's a key point. When you give advice or make product recommendation, explain *why* you think a specific product or action would be best for the customer. Provide pros and cons, a balanced recommendation.

Explain Reasoning or Actions

It's easy to assume that a customer will understand why you're doing something or why you're saying what you're saying. That's a mistake. The customer is not going to be familiar with your company, policies, and procedures, or at least not as familiar as you are.

Explain what you're doing for the customer and *why* you're doing it. Customers want to understand what is going on and may become frustrated or even frightened when they don't understand. Here's a simple example: "I'm going to [explain action] so that you'll be entered in the computer, so next time you come in things will be much faster."

Face-Saving Out

Embarrassing or humiliating a customer is always a bad thing, even in situations where the customer has made a stupid mistake or is angry and unpleasant. Providing a face-saving out is a technique to avoid embarrassing a customer, blaming a customer, or pointing out a customer error or deficiency.

The best way to explain is through example. Let's say a customer appears not to understand what an employee has told him and, even though the employee has given him written material to help him understand, he is still not getting it. The employee could say, "Well, if you read the material you were given, you would understand." That has potential to show up the customer, particularly if that person may have difficulty with reading comprehension. Instead, the employee can offer a face-saving out as follows: "Perhaps the written material isn't very clear or I haven't explained myself well, so let me see if I can talk you through this, since it can get complicated." This removes the blame component by moving responsibility to the employee, while trying not to point out any reading comprehension problems the customer might have.

Finding Agreement Points

When the customer sees you as being "on the same side," he or she is much less likely to strike out at you in anger. One common technique often used in hostage negotiations to create a sense of "we're in it together" is to look for things the customer says that you can agree with. Even expressing agreements on small points, like the weather or other topics not related to why you are talking to the customer, can create a better sense of rapport.

Finishing Off/Following Up

Related to "Arranging Follow-Up," described earlier in this section, following up or finishing off is the process of getting back to a customer to tie up loose ends, confirm that a problem has been solved, or obtain feedback from the customer. When contacting a customer to follow up, it's standard to introduce yourself, explain why you are making the contact, and ask permission to continue or ask if this is a good time. Following up is an extremely important method of showing the customer that he or she is valued and his or her opinions and satisfaction matter.

Isolate/Detach Customer

Isolating or detaching the customer is another name for a process that removes the audience effect (when the customer plays to other customers or bystanders) and provides an opportunity for the customer to think more calmly about the situation and how he or she is behaving. The key issue is to provide time for the customer to think and reflect. See "Timeout" for more details.

Leveling

Leveling involves being honest and forthright without blaming and without strong emotion. It is fairly similar to what some call *assertive communication*. It may involve expressing your feelings about a customer's comments in a calm way or pointing out a customer error in a nonblaming way. It's not a primary customer service technique, except in situations where you have a long-term relationship with a customer that you want to both keep and build. It's best used with customers you know well and you know will respond positively to open and honest communication. Not recommended for customers you do not know well.

Managing Height Differentials/Nonverbals

This involves a family of actions you can take when a customer is intruding into your personal space or using a height advantage and/or body language to intimidate or put you off balance. If you are standing and the customer moves into your space, pivot so you are at a 90-degree angle and not face to face. If you are seated and the customer is standing, it's best to stand. (Get up slowly and calmly.) Often coupled with the distraction technique, the idea is to create a comfort zone for yourself and to move the emphasis from a confrontational position (face to face) to a more cooperative one. With customers who use height differentials and enter your personal space, it's better to use these indirect techniques to manage the situation than to make it an issue by focusing on the space issue verbally.

Managing Interpersonal Distance

We all have comfort zones about our interpersonal space. When a person is too close, it can cause us to feel simply uncomfortable or even threatened and intimidated. All of those feelings make it more difficult to serve the customer. While customers will sometimes enter your interpersonal space intentionally (i.e., getting in your face) because they are angry or frustrated, it may also be unintentional.

Interpersonal space boundaries are both cultural and individual. Some cultures tend to have small interpersonal space (people get closer when they talk); within cultures, individuals differ. What may be uncomfortable for you may be comfortable for the other.

Be that as it may, you need to manage interpersonal distance so you are comfortable. You also want to be aware of the space boundaries of your customers. Don't get too close. If the customer moves backwards or looks away for no apparent reason, you should increase your distance.

If the customer is too close to you, you can use the "90-degree angle" techniques outlined in "Managing Height Differentials/Nonverbals." You can increase distance by directing the person's attention to something (a product or information) that requires the customer to move away from you. Or, of course, you can step away. If you step away, you should do so in a way that sends the message you are stepping toward something and not away from the client. Walk toward a product you are pointing to or to a file you pick up. It's a subtle difference. When you seem to be stepping toward something, it seems less obvious to the customer that you are stepping away from him or her. That's less likely to make interpersonal distance a focal point for your conversation.

Whenever possible, do not make an issue of interpersonal space by referring to it directly and verbally. You really don't want to spend any of your time and the customer's time talking about who is standing where. The exception occurs in some few contexts, such as law enforcement situations and where you are concerned about your physical safety and nothing else works.

However, if you do feel physically threatened, your priority would be to extract yourself immediately.

Not Taking the Bait

One of the simplest techniques, and one of the most important when dealing with an angry customer, not taking the bait means not responding to insults, comments, innuendo, or other angry or abusive comments made by a customer. Typically, you can respond indirectly (using empathy statements) but not respond directly. The key thing to understand is that if you focus on or even simply acknowledge a customer's unpleasant comments, you are going to spend much more time arguing and talking about those comments than you would if you simply ignored them or responded to them with empathy statements. An essential tactic, not taking the bait requires some self-discipline. Remind yourself that the unpleasant customer shouldn't be allowed to upset you or ruin your day, an hour of it, or even a minute. Don't lower yourself to the level of an insulting customer.

Offering Choices/Empowering

One of the major reasons why customers get upset is that they often feel helpless and buffeted by policies, procedures, red tape, and other things they perceive are beyond their control. You can counter this feeling by offering choices to customers whenever possible. By offering them choices, you also show respect for their wishes and help them exert some positive control over the discussions, how and when they occur, and related issues. Even simple things, like offering someone a choice of coffee or tea, can help to create rapport and prevent conflict escalation.

Plain Language

It's easy to forget that our customers do not necessarily understand the jargon, acronyms, and terms that we use every day and take for granted. Using plain language involves translating our language into language that the customer can understand.

For example, a computer technician might use the term "LCD" to refer to a liquid crystal display computer monitor with other technicians, but this term may be totally foreign to most casual computer users. Some will know it, but some will not, so it's good to anticipate that not everyone will understand the term. The technician might translate it into "computer monitor," which is a more familiar term. In addition, the technician should be prepared to explain even that term in simple language. For example, "the computer monitor is the device that you look at when you use the computer." In this example, the technician would use the latter explanation only if the customer seemed to not understand "computer monitor," so as not to insult the customer's knowledge and intelligence.

Another example: A human resource professional might be comfortable using terms like "401(k)" "compensation," and "spousal benefits," but those terms may not be completely clear to an employee. So, the HR employee could replace "401(k)" with "company retirement account," "compensation" with "salary," and "spousal benefits" with "medical insurance for your wife and children." The idea is to focus on clarity and simplicity without being patronizing and to remember to communicate for the benefit of the customer, not yourself.

Preemptive Strike

The term "preemptive strike" is borrowed from the military. In customer service it means anticipating a problem a customer might have and addressing or acknowledging it before the customer brings it up. For example, if a customer has been waiting a long time, you can apologize for the wait or use an empathy statement to show you understand that the customer has been waiting a long time and that he or she is frustrated, rather than wait for the customer to start complaining. By mentioning the problem first, you demonstrate you both understand and are concerned about the customer's feelings. This technique can go a long way to prevent interactions from escalating.

Privacy and Confidentiality

Customers may be concerned about keeping their business and their conversations private, so others don't know about them. When dealing with any details a customer might want kept between the two of you, make sure you do so in an environment where you cannot be overheard *and* make it clear to the customer that you are taking steps to protect his or her privacy and confidentiality. Here's a tip. Some customers want to ensure that their information remains private, even if the information is not what most of us would consider personal. Offer and reassure about privacy and confidentiality, even in situations that might not seem to demand it.

Probing Questions

This technique refers to the use of a series of questions to help clarify a customer's needs, feelings, and wants and the facts of his or her situation. Probing questions are simple ones that cover one issue at a time so as not to overwhelm the customer. The main difference between probing questions and other questions is that a probing question is directly related to the answer the customer provides to the previous question. Probing questions invite the customer to clarify or add to his or her previous response.

For example, "What brought you in today?" is a question. An alternative is to break this down by first saying, "I see you are browsing the plasma television sets. Are you interested in more information about them?" If the customer says yes, the employee probes deeper by asking, "Did you have an interest in a particular size of television?" The interaction may continue this way, with the employee asking simple questions in a series, basing each on the response to earlier questions.

Apart from this being an important tool for getting good information from a customer, it shows that you are listening, since you're basing each question on the specifics of a customer response.

Pros and Cons

Customers see you as more credible or believable when you present both sides of something, like the pros and cons of products. For example, when describing a particular product, it's much better to include both its strengths and its weaknesses relative to other products, rather than to present only its strengths or only its weaknesses. The same applies when explaining any options a customer might have to choose from. Keep in mind that when you present a one-sided view, the customer will wonder why you are presenting what may appear to be an unbalanced perspective and will question or suspect your motives.

Providing Alternatives

Similar to "providing choices/empowering," this is a simple technique to present possible alternative products, services, or actions that might apply to the customer's situation. For example, "You can contact me by phone or e-mail, whatever is more convenient" provides two alternatives to the customer. What's the difference between offering choices, as described earlier, and offering alternatives? When you offer choices, you usually ask the customer which alternatives he or she wants to pursue. Providing alternatives demonstrates your interest in ensuring that the customer understands his or her options.

Providing a Customer Takeaway

Providing a customer takeaway involves giving something physical to the customer to take away. For example, you might provide a brochure, product information, a phone number written down that a customer needs, or a list of steps for a customer to solve a problem. When you provide a takeaway, you are not forcing the customer to rely on his or her memory and the customer can refer to it if needed. If you don't have printed material available, you can write down notes for the customer to take away. This is often seen by customers as being helpful beyond their expectations, which is a good thing. Takeaways can also be brief summaries of a conversation.

Providing Explanations

You may be surprised at the idea that employees tend to take for granted that customers understand what the employees are saying. But it happens all the time. Providing explanations means exactly what you'd think it means: you explain. Here's an example. Let's say a customer wants to return some underwear, but your store does not accept such returns for hygienic reasons. You could assume the reasoning is obvious, which would be a mistake, or you could explain the reasoning by talking about why your store has that policy, referencing any laws that might apply or that the policy exists to protect every customer.

When you educate a customer, that person usually becomes a better customer, easier to serve, and more loyal.

Questioning Instead of Stating

Questions can sometimes be used to soften a statement or command. Let's say a customer has a complaint about something. You could say, "Go down the hall and speak to our customer service branch." But that statement sounds harsh, because it's a command. People don't like to be ordered around. So, you can use a question to soften the situation like this: "Were you aware that you can speak to our customer service branch and they'll be able to help you?" In effect you are saying almost exactly the same thing, but the question form comes across as much more cooperative and avoids giving the impression that you are ordering the customer around.

Referral to Supervisor

There are situations when you are unable to help a customer further because you lack the authority or information to do so. There are other situations where a customer, usually angry, will likely respond more politely if he or she can talk with someone perceived as having more status in the organization—a manager or supervisor. We know that when a customer talks with a supervisor or someone else with more status he or she tends to behave more civilly than with someone seen as having less status.

Whether you cannot help due to lack of authority and information or whether you feel the customer will respond more positively with a supervisor, the techniques used are the same. First, ask or confirm that the customer wants to speak with the supervisor. Second, contact the supervisor and explain the situation to him or her. Normally you would provide the supervisor with the customer's name, the problem or issue, and the customer's general state of mind. This step ensures that the supervisor isn't blindsided, eliminates any need for the customer to explain the entire situation, and allows the supervisor to take control of the interaction when he or she makes contact with the customer.

Finally, the supervisor is "connected" with the customer. This might involve the supervisor introducing himself or herself as follows: "Hi, I'm Ms. Jones, and I understand you have some concerns about your billing." Whether the supervisor initiates contact in person or on the phone, the procedure should be the same.

It's absolutely important that you and your supervisor are on the same wavelength on referrals. Some supervisors don't ever want to have customers referred to them, some are willing under certain circumstances, and others are much more open. You need to know what *your* supervisor expects—and the time to find out is not when you have an angry customer waiting. Ask your supervisor when it's OK to refer customers and how he or she wants the process handled. Then abide by those wishes.

Referral to Third Party

This technique is very similar to "referral to supervisor," except that the person who will receive the customer isn't a supervisor, but someone else in the organization, often a coworker. Third-party referrals are useful when someone else may know more about the subject at hand than you do or when you believe that someone else, because of his or her personal style or approach, might work more effectively with a specific customer. Referral to a third party can also be used when a supervisor is not available.

The process works exactly the same, except that you present the third party as someone who is expert or knowledgeable, to enhance his or her perceived status. For example: "You might prefer to talk to John Angus. He's the person who knows the most about [subject of interest to customer]." Again, ensure that you inform the third party about the customer's situation before he or she interacts with the customer.

Refocus

Refocusing a conversation means bringing it back to the original issue or topic. Let's say an angry customer has a complaint about a product or service. He starts off talking about the problem, but then starts making critical remarks about the company or about you personally. Those comments and discussing them in depth are not going to help the customer resolve his concern. What you do is couple an empathy statement with a refocus statement as follows. "I can see you are angry about the product problem. Let's get back to what we can do to help you. I can suggest a few things that might help." What you want to do is shift the customer's attention away from his anger, and to something more constructive.

Setting Limits

You set limits in situations where a customer is acting in nonconstructive ways. The customer might be raising his or her voice, swearing, or making repeated nuisance phone calls. In order to help the customer (and keep your sanity), you need to encourage the customer to stop the inappropriate or destructive behavior. There are several parts to setting limits.

The setting limits process begins with an "if … then" statement. In that statement you are going to identify as specifically as possible what behavior you want to stop. You are also going to identify the consequence that will occur if the customer does not stop. It sounds like this: "If you do not stop swearing, I'm going to have to end this conversation." Here, the behavior is "swearing" and the consequence is "end this conversation."

But you aren't finished yet. The next step is to provide a choice statement. So after the "if … then" step, you add, "It's up to you whether you'd like to continue."

This step is included because we want the customer to understand that he gets to decide whether to stop swearing (and continue the conversation) or continue swearing (and end the conversation). By framing it as a choice for the customer, the consequence seems less like something the employee does *to* the customer and less like a punishment.

You must handle the entire process of setting limits and enforcing them calmly, so it does not seem like the process is personal.

If the customer abides by the limit, then the conversation can continue. If the customer continues to swear or argue, then the conversation must be terminated. Here's what you would say on the phone. "I'm going to end this conversation now. You are welcome to call back at some other time." You include the last sentence to tell the customer that you will be glad to help at some other time—provided that he stops swearing. Once you've indicated you are ending the conversation, you will do so unless the customer offers a clear apology or commitment to abide by the limit you set.

Before using limits to end interactions, you should be clear about your organization's policies and wishes regarding what constitutes reasonable grounds for ending an interaction or refusing further service. Also remember that setting and enforcing limits should be a last resort: use it only after other techniques have failed to encourage the customer to act more constructively.

Some People Think That (Neutral Mode)

Neutral mode is an indirect way to acknowledge something a customer has said without agreeing with it or disagreeing with it. That's why it's called neutral mode. Because it's an unusual, novel, or unexpected response, the technique tends to interrupt the flow of anger or emotion and causes the customer to stop and think. This provides the employee with an opening to use other techniques.

This technique has a specific form. If you change it much, it doesn't work as well. It goes like this: "Some people do think that [rephrase what the customer said in a straightforward, dispassionate way.]"

Let's say a customer is going on and on about how inefficient government is. The employee, wanting to interrupt the flow, or rant, says, "You know, some people do feel that government isn't as efficient as it might be."

Notice that the employee didn't say "wastes money" or "squanders money" or any other stronger, emotionally laden words. That's important. Always rephrase in a neutral, unemotional way.

When the technique works, the customer will respond with a short sentence or two, then stop. Then the employee uses other techniques to intervene and get control over the conversation. The two most important techniques coupled with "neutral mode" are "Empathy Statements" and "Refocus."

Stop Sign—Nonverbal

Do you need to get an in-person customer to stop and listen? You can use the nonverbal stop sign to indicate you'd like to say something. The technique is simple, but you need to execute it just right. Hold up your hand toward the customer, with the palm facing half toward the floor and half toward the customer. In other words, your hand should be at about a 45-degree angle. Ensure that you are far enough away from the customer that there will be no risk of physical contact. Keep your hand no higher than the customer's chest level, not in his or her face.

This technique should *not* be used with any customer who appears potentially violent. Also, the stop sign should be raised slowly, not abruptly, and it can be coupled with a simple verbal request (e.g., "Hold on a sec.").

Suggest an Alternative to Waiting

This technique is an extension of the "Providing Alternatives" technique mentioned earlier. When customers are waiting, let's say in a doctor's waiting room, the longer they wait, the angrier they get. One reason is they don't know what to do. Do they have to stay in the waiting room or risk losing their places? Can they go somewhere and come back? Is there time to grab a cup of coffee?

If you are in charge of the waiting room, it's good to both explain the reasons for the delay and suggest what customers might do while they wait. Or, indicate they can reschedule if waiting is a problem. A very useful example goes like this: "For those of you with appointments after three o'clock, feel free to step out for a coffee break or snack in the restaurant next door. Just be sure to be back within a half-hour of your scheduled appointment and you won't lose your spot."

Summarize the Conversation

A simple technique used either in the middle or at the end of a conversation, this involves doing a quick recap of the critical parts of the discussion. Summarize any important details and particularly any specific commitments you and/or your customer have made during the conversation.

Summarizing shows that you are paying attention, but there's a more important reason to use it. It's not uncommon during conversations for both parties to believe that they understand what is being said in exactly the same way. But they may not. If misunderstandings are not caught, serious problems can arise. Summarizing allows you to confirm with the customer that both you and he or she understand what has been said in the same way.

Summarizing verbally can be accompanied by providing the customer with a takeaway—a written summary of the conversation.

Telephone Silence

It's sometimes hard to get someone on the phone to be quiet and listen to you, so you can offer help. Some people talk incessantly when they are upset, angry, frustrated, or frightened. One of the best ways to get a customer to stop talking over the phone is to say absolutely nothing. No words. No "Uh-huh." Nothing. What will happen is that the customer will stop and ask, "Hello, hello, are you there?" and then wait for a response from you. That gives you an opening to use other techniques and get some control over the conversation.

If you have a mute button, that works even better, because it blocks out all sounds, including background noise. Do *not* put a customer on hold in this situation. Putting a customer on hold means you cannot hear them or know when they have stopped talking so you can jump into the gap to take some control of the conversation. The mute button allows you to hear the customer, but the customer cannot hear you or any background noise.

Thank-Yous

One of the most obvious and simple techniques needs little explanation. Everyone likes to be thanked. Thank people. One tip: don't just say, "Thank you"—be more specific. For example, "Thank you for being so patient" or "Thank you for visiting our company."

Timeout

You might be familiar with timeouts in relation to children who are acting out. The principles are similar for adults: the timeout can provide a cooling-off period for customers who are upset or angry, particularly if their anger is getting in the way of providing help to them. Basically, you provide some sensible reason why the customer should wait on his or her own for a minute or two, preferably in a locale away from other people. For example, if you were in an office with a customer, you could say, "I need to check to make sure what I'm saying is accurate. Let me do that. It will just take a minute." Then exit, leaving the customer alone. Return in a minute or two.

Most angry customers are regular people who are upset and acting aggressively only temporarily. When you give them the chance to think about what they are doing, they will often apologize to you and act more constructively.

It's important to keep the timeout short. If it goes past a few minutes, that may provide an additional reason for the customer to remain angry or even for the anger to escalate. It's also important to understand that timeouts, at least for adults, are *not* punitive. They are meant to provide time to think.

Use Customer's Name

Another simple technique requires little explanation, using the customer's name personalizes the service you provide and indicates you think the customer is important enough to remember his or her name. There's another advantage: it indirectly suggests the customer is not anonymous. Anonymity tends to increase aggression.

It is sometimes difficult to know how to address a customer. With a woman, do you use Ms., Mrs., or Miss? When do you use a first name? The best way to find out is to ask how a customer would prefer to be addressed. First names are best used with customers you know well.

Use of Timing with Angry Customers

We've included this technique because timing is so important when dealing with angry customers. It's not a technique so much as something you should be aware of. Angry people are often not ready or even able to think logically or in an organized way. If you try to solve a customer's problem when he or she is not ready, it won't work.

First, deal with the customer's feelings using various acknowledgment and empathy techniques. Only when the customer is acting less upset should you move on (refocus) to solve the specific problem.

Here's a tip. You will know you are problem-solving too early if the customer ignores your attempts and you have to repeat yourself because he or she isn't hearing you.

Verbal Softeners

People don't respond well to language that sounds absolute, authoritarian, or harsh. For example, "We never make those kinds of mistakes" is very categorical and likely to antagonize even mild-mannered customers. Here's another way of putting it: "It's unlikely we've made a mistake." The word "unlikely" is a verbal softener. Other softeners include *perhaps, sometimes, it's possible*, and *occasionally*.

Here's another example, in a situation where the employee believes the customer has made a mistake. He could say, "Clearly, you've made a mistake." That would be bad. He could soften the sentence by saying, "Perhaps you've misinterpreted something here." "Perhaps" is the softener, but notice we've also replaced the word "mistake" with "misinterpreted," a less harsh word.

Verbal softeners are exceedingly valuable tools to help you appear more cooperative and likeable to customers and to prevent conflict from arising from the use of harsh language.

Voice Tone—Emphatic

You can use an emphatic voice tone to convey that you are strongly committed to helping the customer. For example, let's say a customer has been telling you that he's late for an appointment and is double-parked and needs to be served quickly. You can respond in a laidback way, but it's better to respond more emphatically—"*I understand, I will* get this done for you!" Note the emphasis on "will." Emphatic voice tones work best when they match the tone and energy that the customer is using.

When Question

The "when question" is a cousin of "neutral mode." Its function is to force the customer to think, thereby interrupting the flow of angry or aggressive speech aimed at you. It works on the same principle. The "when question" is an unusual or novel question and it's closed-ended so it tends to elicit short answers, which are what you want. It also has a specific form that goes like this:

"When did you start thinking that [summarize in a neutral way a key point from what the customer said]?"

When this works properly, the customer will respond with a specific time or incident and then stop. That gives you the opening you need so you can use other techniques.

So, let's say the customer is accusing you of not caring. He says: "If you gave a damn about me, you'd take care of me properly."

The employee replies, "When did you start feeling you weren't getting the service you wanted?"

The customer answers, "The first time I came in here," and then stops talking.

The employee uses that opening to empathize and try to refocus the customer back to the issue and back to more constructive behavior.

It's very important, once again, to not repeat any hot or emotional words the customer uses. For example, it would not work if the employee said, "When did you start thinking I didn't give a damn about you?"

You're Right!

The "you're right!" technique is a cousin of "neutral mode," the "when question," and "finding agreement points." It serves to surprise an angry customer, since the last thing he or she expects in the middle of a rant is for you to say "You're right!" You'll find that emphatic use of this phrase will result in the customer not knowing what to say next. That provides an opening for you to use other techniques.

The "you're right!" method is more emphatic than "finding agreement points."

Part Two

Dealing with Specific Customer Situations

1. When You Are Late or Know You Will Be Late

THE SITUATION

Being late for an appointment or meeting with a customer is not a good thing, but there are situations where you are delayed a) due to circumstances beyond your control or b) because you needed to do something for the benefit of the customer. Here are some tips on how to handle situations where you know you will be late or you actually arrive late.

TECHNIQUES USED

- Apologize (1)
- Explain Reasoning or Actions (2)
- Empathy Statements (3)
- Offering Choices/Empowering (4)
- Providing Alternatives (5)
- Thank-Yous (6)

DIALOGUE

The employee realizes he is going to be at least 10 minutes late for a meeting with his customers because there was a delay in printing material that is needed for the meeting. The employee contacts the customer by phone.

Employee: Mr. Jones, I'm really sorry. (1) It looks like I'm going to be about 10 minutes late to arrive because there's been a delay in printing out the contracts we need to look at during the meeting. (2) I'm printing them out now and shouldn't be later than 3 p.m. (2)

Customer: Well, I've got the VP of Finance coming and I can't have him sitting around waiting. I have to tell you I'm not impressed.

Employee: I can understand you are disappointed. (3) I had to decide whether to delay coming over until the contracts are done or to come on time without the contracts. (2) It seems like the best use of time, but if you want to reschedule or if there's any way to make this more convenient, I'm flexible. (4)

Customer: No, that's fine.

Employee: If you want to go over the other reports while you're waiting, maybe we can shorten the meeting. (5)

Customer: That's a good idea.

When the employee finally arrives, this is what he says.

Employee: I have to apologize to all of you, (1) and especially to Mr. Smith (VP of Finance), for being late, and thank you for your patience. (6) [He then explains the reason for arriving late.] (2)

EXPLANATIONS

Most of the techniques used in this example are straightforward. The use of apologies (1), thank-yous (6), and empathy statements (3) doesn't need additional explanation.

Here's what's important. Even though the delay is "only" 10 minutes, the employee notifies the customer of the delay and provides an explanation of why he will be late. (2) Notification, even when you will only be a few minutes late, is always a good thing, because it demonstrates your concern for the customer and his or her time. If you look at (4), you will see the use of offering a choice to the customer. He is offering an "out" so that if the customer needs to reschedule or cancel the meeting, he can do so using the opening the employee provides.

In (5), the employee offers an alternative or suggestion as to how the customer might use the 10-minute delay to his advantage, recognizing that the delay shouldn't create "dead time" for the others attending the meeting.

Finally, when the employee arrives, you can see a repeat of the techniques the employee used when notifying the customer of the delay. The employee decides to explain why he is late just in case the people attending the meeting were not informed of the reason for the delay.

HINTS

If you are late without good reason (e.g., oversleeping, error in planning), it's probably best to give only a limited and general explanation, such as "I was unavoidably detained," or to be honest and admit your mistake. The more established and positive your relationships with the customer, the more honest you can be.

See Also: 9. When the Customer Has Been Through Voicemail Hell, 11. When the Customer Has Been "Buck-Passed"

2. When a Customer Is in a Hurry

THE SITUATION

In this day and age, people and customers are often in a hurry to conduct their business and move on. How can you interact with a customer who is in a hurry in a way that reflects that you understand the customer's need for speed?

TECHNIQUES USED

- Voice Tone—Emphatic (1)
- Assurances of Results (2)

DIALOGUE

A customer arrives at an airline counter to check in for her flight and is clearly flustered, out of breath, and in a hurry.

Customer: Oh lord, I don't want to miss my flight, my car broke down, and oh goodness ….

Employee: We'll get you on your flight. (2) [She looks at the ticket the customer presents.] No problem. You still have 15 minutes to get to the gate (1, 2). Bags to check? (1)

Customer: Just the one.

Employee: Seat preference, aisle or window? (1)

Customer: Window.

EXPLANATIONS

Since the customer is clearly flustered, the employee first reassures the customer that she won't miss her flight in (2). In addition to that simple reassurance, the employee informs the customer that she still has 15 minutes to get to the gate. That's reassuring information.

What really works well here is the use of a tone of voice that matches the situation. The employee uses a very firm, emphatic tone of voice (1), but also speaks more quickly than normal and in shorter sentences than she would with someone who is not feeling so time-pressured. Why? By speaking in a way that conveys urgency, she is communicating to the customer that she understands the customer's situation and is modifying her behavior to address the customer's need.

HINTS

The way you speak (speed, intensity, length) is important in conveying the right message to a customer. The key is to modify how you speak to fit the context. In this example, the employee speaks more quickly, more intensely, and in short bursts to reflect the urgency of the situation. In a funeral home, this way of speaking would be completely inappropriate. A slower, calmer, and more empathetic tone would fit.

See Also: 3. When a Customer Jumps Ahead in a Line of Waiting Customers, 4. When a Customer Asks to Be Served Ahead of Other Waiting Customers

3. When a Customer Jumps Ahead in a Line of Waiting Customers

THE SITUATION

One of the most frustrating things for customers is when someone pushes ahead of them in a line and for the employee to serve the more aggressive customer first, ignoring the fact that the aggressive customer has pushed in. To ignore the situation almost ensures that the customer being delayed is going to blame the employee for the aggressive customer's rude or oblivious behavior.

TECHNIQUES USED

- Verbal Softeners (1)
- Face-Saving Out (2)

DIALOGUE

This situation could occur in any context where people line up for service—grocery stores, other retail establishments, banks, hotels, restaurants. There's a line of five people waiting to be served and a sixth person steps into the middle of the line. Before any of the other customers says anything, the employee intervenes.

Employee: [to the customer who has pushed in] Perhaps you didn't notice that the line actually ends after this gentleman. (1) If you could move to the end, I'll be glad to serve you in turn.

Customer: Oh, I'm sorry. I didn't see that.

Employee: No problem. It's easy to miss. (2)

EXPLANATIONS

In this situation it's important to point out that the customer has jumped the line without doing anything that might humiliate or embarrass him or her. In (1) the employee uses a very gentle way of letting the customer know about the line, careful not to accuse the customer. The word "perhaps" is a good example of a verbal softener. Notice the difference in tone between what the employee said and the following: "Hey, you jumped the line. Get back to the end." Quite different.

In (2), you can see an example of a similar technique, providing a face-saving out. Since the customer has apologized, the employee can soften any embarrassment by making it OK, indicating that it's a mistake that's easy to make. That ends the interaction on a positive note.

HINTS

It's important that an employee who deals with situations where customers line up make a conscious effort to monitor the line in order to address "pushing-in" issues before another customer does. You don't want two customers arguing about something that is ultimately your responsibility.

When a customer cuts in, you can't know whether it is an intentional act of rudeness and inconsideration or simply a result of inattention. For this reason, you should always give the benefit of the doubt. To accuse a customer of pushing in intentionally is almost always guaranteed to start an argument. Even if you have a strong suspicion it was intentional, you must start with a gentle approach.

See Also: 2. When a Customer Is in a Hurry, 5. When a Customer Interrupts a Discussion Between the Employee and Another Customer

4. When a Customer Asks to Be Served Ahead of Other Waiting Customers

THE SITUATION

Here's a situation you may have encountered if you work in a retail environment. A customer in a line up at the cash register asks whether she can be served without waiting, because she is either in a hurry, or feels that her small number of items somehow justifies moving ahead of people with many more items to be processed at the check-out. Denying the request may incur the ire of the customer requesting the "speed-up" while accommodating the request may alienate the people ahead of her in the line. What do you do?

TECHNIQUES USED

■ Offering Choices/Empowering (1)

DIALOGUE

Four people are waiting in line at a grocery store. The first three people have full baskets while the fourth person has only three items. The customer with the fewest items gets your attention and asks if she can go first.

Customer: I'm in a real hurry and I only have a few items, so can I go ahead of these people?

Employee: Since these people have been waiting longer and might also be in a rush, it's really up to them. (1) If they don't mind, I can take you first. Otherwise, the wait is only a few minutes.

Customer: [to others in the line] Does anyone mind if I go ahead of you?

EXPLANATIONS

The cashier could have made a judgment call in this situation and simply made the decision himself, but that would have put the cashier in the middle—really between a rock and a hard place. Instead, the employee turns the responsibility for the decision back to where it belongs—to the people who might be inconvenienced. He provides the opportunity for the customer in a hurry to ask the others (1), if she chooses to do so. It's then up to the other customers. Not only is that the fairest way to deal with this situation, but it also sends the message that the customers who have been waiting are important to the employee.

HINTS

Notice that the cashier doesn't volunteer to ask the other customers himself. He puts the onus (and the choice) to do so on the customer who wants to be served first. Another reason for doing it this way is that it helps the other customers see the employee as neutral on this issue.

In situations like this, the employee needs to have a unanimous "vote" in order to break with procedure. A majority vote is not enough to change the order/procedure.

See Also: 2. When a Customer Is in a Hurry, 4. When a Customer Asks to Be Served Ahead of Other Waiting Customers

5. When a Customer Interrupts a Discussion Between the Employee and Another Customer

THE SITUATION

You may face a situation where you are helping one customer and a second customer rushes up and interrupts your conversation. It may appear that you are caught between a rock and a hard place, since if you serve the first customer, the second may become annoyed, and if you serve the second one, the first customer, quite justifiably, may feel you are not treating him or her as important. In this situation we'll describe a single technique—the "stop sign—nonverbal" tactic.

TECHNIQUES USED

■ Stop Sign—Nonverbal (1)

DIALOGUE

In a retail store, the employee has been talking with a primary customer for three or four minutes. All of a sudden, a second customer rushes up and interrupts the conversation.

Second Customer: Excuse me, but can you tell me who I need to talk to about returning some merchandise?

Employee: [turns to the second customer, makes eye contact, and holds up hand at about a 45-degree angle toward the second customer] I can help you in just a moment or you can go to the service desk. [The employee then breaks eye contact and returns to the first customer.] (1)

EXPLANATIONS

The first priority is always the customer with whom you're interacting. The key is to limit your interaction with the interrupting customer, so it's as brief as possible. That's why the employee uses a very short sentence and then immediately returns his attention to the first customer, indicating this by shifting eye contact. Note also that the employee, in his short sentence with the second customer, offers an option—wait or go to the service desk.

HINTS

Generally, you should not address the needs of the interrupting customer even if you can address them quickly, because it sends a message that the first customer is less important.

As an additional technique, if you feel you can address the second customer's concerns quickly, you could ask the first customer for permission to do so as follows: "Do you mind if I help this fellow out while you look at the items you are interested in? It will only take 30 seconds or so."

See Also: 2. When a Customer Is in a Hurry, 3. When a Customer Jumps Ahead in a Line of Waiting Customers

THE SITUATION

You may come across a situation where your customer comes in with a "chip on his shoulder" because he believes he has been treated badly in the past or has heard from others that your organization doesn't treat people well. This tends to happen more often in government and public sector environments (e.g., schools) because, unlike in the private sector, the customer cannot simply go somewhere else. The person needs to deal with the specific organization and the organization needs to provide service. How do you deal with the customer with negative preconceptions, whether justified or not?

TECHNIQUES USED

- Active Listening (1)
- Not Taking the Bait (2)
- Some People Think That (neutral mode) (3)
- Assurances of Effort (4)
- Refocus (5)

DIALOGUE

This situation occurs in a government office. The customer can't choose to take his business elsewhere and clearly has some negative preconceptions.

Customer: OK. I need to get these building permits done, and I don't want you guys to jerk me around like you usually do or run me through reams of red tape. I don't have the time.

Employee: It sounds to me like you want to get these permits done as quickly as possible, right? (1, 2)

Customer: Damn right. You know, nobody likes dealing with you guys. It's always a major hassle, and you screw it up half the time.

Employee: Some people get impatient with the process. (3) Let's see if I can surprise you. (4) Since you want to get this done fast, let's get to it. (5) I know you've done this before, so you probably have the information you need for the permits? (5)

EXPLANATIONS

Before we go through the specifics, what attitude is the employee demonstrating? Is it defensive? Or is the employee seeing this situation as a challenge he can win, turning around the negative attitude? Clearly, it's the latter. It's important that you do not feel defensive, argue, or react in negative ways.

Take a look at the first employee response. The employee wants to show concern, demonstrate she has heard the customer's comments, but not encourage the customer to rant and rave about the government organization. She does this by using a listening response (1) and by not taking the bait, and arguing with the customer to get him to change his mind about government.

The employee continues to acknowledge the concerns without encouraging in-depth focusing on his negative impressions by using a "when" question, sometimes called neutral mode ("Some people think that ") (3). This shows that she is paying attention, without encouraging argument.

In (4) she indicates that she will try to offer a better experience (assurances of effort). Then in (5) she makes the important transition away from the negative feelings to address the reason why the customer has come in—the permits. That's refocusing.

HINTS

As with all situations in which the customer is angry or prepared to be angry, it's important to acknowledge (show you hear and understand) "where the customer is coming from," without necessarily agreeing or disagreeing. However, you don't want to spend more time than is necessary on the feelings or the past. Acknowledge, then refocus on the task at hand.

Apart from refocusing from anger to the task, also refocus (move the conversation) from what's happened in the past to what's in front of the both of you—the here and now. Since customers usually want something now, it's to their benefit to stop focusing on the bad things they think have been done to them in the past and focus on getting things done in the present. That makes it easy to make the case for talking about the present and what you can do now for the customer.

See Also: 8. When a Customer Might Be Mistrustful, 54. When a Customer Complains About Red Tape and Paperwork

7. When You Need to Explain a Company Policy or Procedure

THE SITUATION

In an ideal world, your customers would already understand your policies and procedures and be willing to abide by them. But we don't live in an ideal world.

Whether it's a policy regarding returns of merchandize in the retail sector or a policy regarding who can receive specific government services, it's often the case that customers don't understand why those policies and procedures are in place. A customer who doesn't understand the purpose of a policy is much more likely to become angry if he or she sees the policy as interfering with getting what he or she wants. If you can explain the policy and the reasoning behind it so the customer understands, you are much less likely to receive flak about the policy.

TECHNIQUES USED

- Preemptive Strike (1)
- Plain Language (2)
- Providing a Customer Takeaway (3)

DIALOGUE

This example occurs in a government office, although similar situations could occur in any other sector. The customer is asked to furnish some information so his application can be processed. Unless the customer provides the information, his application can't be processed, because the policy requires this information. We join the conversation after the customer has made his original request.

Employee: I know this is going to be frustrating, but in order to process your application, we need to have some proof of identity, really two pieces of I.D. (1) One needs to have your picture on it. We also need proof of residence.

Customer: Darn right, it's frustrating. Why are you putting me through all these hoops? It's just typical of bureaucracy that I have to fill in umpteen forms and give you all kinds of personal information.

Employee: Maybe it would help if I explain why we need this information. Then it will make more sense. The major reason we ask for this information is to make sure that nobody can steal your identity and make an application using your identity. That's why we need positive proof so we are absolutely sure that nobody can do that. It's for everyone's protection. (2)

Customer: Well, OK. What exactly do you accept?

Employee: We accept a number of documents and I have a pamphlet that lists acceptable identification that you can keep. But let's go over the documents you can use. (3)

EXPLANATIONS

In this example, the employee knows that customers tend to resent having to provide the necessary documents. To cushion the blow, the employee uses the preemptive strike (1) to acknowledge that the customer may feel upset about the requirements. The premise here is that it's better for the employee to broach the subject of frustration, rather than wait for the customer to do so first.

Notice how the employee explains the purpose of the requirement. She explains it (2) in very plain language and from the point of view of the customer. When explaining policy, it's best to highlight how the policy benefits the customer and to avoid sounding bureaucratic.

In (3) she offers some printed material to the customer, a "takeaway." Why? So the customer doesn't have to rely only on his memory for critical information. The customer will be able to use this material to prepare if he has to come back. Also, note that the employee goes over the takeaway with the customer and doesn't rely on him actually reading the document.

HINTS

When explaining policy, it's best not to quote a specific policy number, clause, or detail from a policy manual. Policies and procedures are usually not written with the customer in mind and the language can be excessively bureaucratic. Also, it tends to suggest that your focus is on policies and procedures rather than people.

Rephrase the policy in plain language.

If you don't know the rationale behind a policy or procedure, you can offer to find out for the customer.

See Also: 54. When a Customer Complains About Red Tape and Paperwork, 60. When a Customer Tries an Unacceptable Merchandise Return

8. When a Customer Might Be Mistrustful

THE SITUATION

A customer who mistrusts you is going to be a difficult customer. Some professions or fields tend to garner more mistrust than others, primarily because the customer lacks the information to determine if you are serving him or her, or being self-serving. The techniques in this example are designed to build customer confidence in your honesty.

TECHNIQUES USED

- Explain Reasoning or Actions (1)
- Acknowledge Customer's Needs (2)
- Pros and Cons (3)
- Expert Recommendations (4)

DIALOGUE

In this example, a car mechanic is explaining the problems found with the customer's vehicle. The employee realizes the customer might mistrust what he's saying and takes action to build confidence.

Employee: As part of our normal vehicle check, we do a 45-point inspection in addition to looking at the reason why you brought the car in. We should talk about some of the other things you might want to address. (1)

Customer: [sounds dubious] OK.

Employee: Since you mentioned trouble with your brakes, that was the first thing we looked at. We found that the brake pads are 90% worn on the front. We also noticed you have a small oil leak. (1)

Customer: [Puts hand on chin, shakes head]

Employee: I'm thinking you want to keep repair costs down, since this is an older vehicle (2). So, I'd suggest that we replace the brake pads because [explains safety reasons] (4). Regarding the oil leak, to tell you the truth it's probably not worth repairing it. The advantage to addressing the leak is that you may save a bit of money on oil. (3) The disadvantage is that repairing the leak will involve taking the engine apart to replace a gasket. That's expensive. In any event, most older vehicles leak some oil. (3)

So, I'd suggest we do the brakes and keep an eye on the leak. If it gets worse down the road, we can discuss it again. (4)

EXPLANATIONS

The idea here is that the mechanic is presenting himself as working on behalf of the customer and not trying to pad the bill. First, he explains the process by which he identified the oil leak (1). Next, he proves to the customer that he understands his concerns and needs by acknowledging those needs (2).

The most important part of this interaction lies with presenting pros and cons from the customer's point of view (3). By presenting reasons why it may not be worthwhile to address the oil leak, the employee shows that he is acting in the interests of the customer, while leaving the door open for the customer to decide to have it repaired.

Finally, we see the employee offer his expert opinions about what should be done.

HINTS

Don't assume that a customer understands the pros and cons of various options. Often they don't and they want your expert (and honest, balanced) opinion.

Presenting both pros and cons is critical to developing customer confidence in your honesty.

See Also: 6. When a Customer Has a Negative Attitude About Your Company Due to Past Experiences, 7. When You Need to Explain a Company Policy or Procedure

9. When the Customer Has Been Through Voicemail Hell

THE SITUATION

These days most companies use some form of voicemail or automated phone system. Unfortunately, these systems are not always well thought out, resulting in situations where a customer can be routed around and around without having his or her needs met in a timely and simple manner. How can you deal with an irate customer who has had the misfortune of spending frustrating time navigating a voicemail or automated system and has now connected with you?

TECHNIQUES USED

- Assurances of Effort (1)
- Apologize (2)
- You're Right! (3)
- Offering Choices/Empowering (4)
- Broken Record (5)
- Refocus (6)

DIALOGUE

In this situation the customer is trying to get help with a computer problem he's experiencing. He's been through a number of "phone menus" and has been unable to reach a human or voicemail. (The mailbox is full.) He finally figures out how to speak to a live human being—you—and he's exceedingly annoyed.

Customer: What the heck is wrong with you people? I've been going around and around in your voicemail system and I haven't been able to even leave a voicemail so I can get some help. I should be able to contact you without having to spend all my money on long-distance charges.

Employee: I am going to help you (1) and I apologize if you've been having problems with our phone system. (2) You're right that this shouldn't happen. (3) Since you've already spent so much time on the phone, can I ask you a few questions so I can help? (4, 6)

Customer: Damn right this shouldn't happen! I need help and I need it right away, and I don't deserve to be going around in circles.

Employee: You're right. (2, 5) I'm sure you want that help *now*, so let me ask you some questions. Are you calling about a technical problem with a computer? (4, 6)

Customer: Yes.

Employee: OK. If you give me the make and model number and the nature of the problem, I can transfer you directly to a live person who can help.

EXPLANATIONS

This interaction follows a tried-and-true pattern for dealing with irate customers. The first goal is to defuse the customer's anger. Once the customer has calmed down a little bit, the employee moves the customer away from the secondary issue (frustration with the phone system) and back to the reason the customer called (technical problem).

The defusing process uses a succession of techniques, including assurances the employee will help (1), an apology (2), and the "you're right" technique (3).

As is often the case, the customer doesn't respond

immediately and constructively, so the employee uses the broken record technique several times (4, 6).

Pay special attention to the use of refocus techniques. The refocus (4, 6) is used to focus the customer away from his anger and back to the reason why he called. In this case, the employee uses questions for this purpose and asks for permission to help the customer (4, 6) (offering choices/empowerment).

HINTS

When interacting with an angry customer, you will almost always have to defuse (deal with the anger) before you can move on to why the person is calling (the initial issue). That's because angry people are not ready to problem-solve. So, the first step is to use defusing techniques *first*.

The refocus technique is a key element for making the transition from focusing on anger to focusing on the needs of the customer. If a refocus statement or question does not work initially, it can be repeated (broken record), using different words.

Needless to say, it's absolutely critical that the customer not be returned to the "voicemail from hell" system, only to repeat the frustrating experience. When rescuing someone from the voicemail nightmare, find a way to avoid sending the person back to the voicemail (e.g., take a paper message, arrange a follow-up callback manually).

See Also: 11. When a Customer Has Been "Buck-Passed," 14. When a Customer Won't Stop Talking on the Phone

10. When a Customer Is Experiencing a Language Barrier

THE SITUATION

One of the biggest challenges in customer service involves dealing with a customer who has trouble understanding how you talk or is difficult to understand. While you'd think this happens primarily when dealing with someone born in another country and whose mother tongue is different from yours, it can also happen when people with different accents are talking.

TECHNIQUES USED

- Plain Language (1)
- Probing Questions (2)
- Summarize the Conversation (3)

DIALOGUE

In this example, the customer appears to be having difficulty making his needs understood because his native tongue is other than English. In addition, he seems to be having difficulty understanding what the employee is saying.

Customer: [asks employee a question that employee does not understand]

Employee: [talks slowly, calmly] I'm not sure I know how to help. Do you want help with insurance? (1, 2)

Customer: Yes, insurance.

Employee: OK, good. Car insurance? (1, 2)

Customer: No, no car.

Employee: House insurance? (1, 2)

Customer: Yes, yes.

Employee: OK. You own a house and you need insurance? (1, 3)

EXPLANATIONS

There is no easy solution to language barriers. Obviously the best solution is to connect the customer with some-one who can speak his or her language or who might be better at understanding the specific accent, but that's not always practical.

In this example the strategy is clear. Throughout, the employee uses some plain language strategies (1). In par-ticular, he breaks down the conversation into smaller "bits" and short sentences and questions. Here's why. A person struggling to understand another language has a lot to think about. It helps if he or she has to think about only one small thing at a time.

You can also see the use of probing questions (2), which in this case are short and can be answered with either a yes or a no. Again, this is to try to make the com-munication process simpler.

In (3) you can see the employee summarizing the conversation so far. In effect, he is checking with the cus-tomer to verify that they are both understanding the con-versation.

HINTS

Perhaps the most important aspect of dealing with a lan-guage barrier is patience. Remember that it's frustrating for both of you, but that it's *your* job to make sure the com-munication works. Avoid any and all signs of frustration.

Don't speak more loudly. When there is a language barrier, people tend to yell, which would make you look completely foolish, startle the other person, and possibly even antagonize him or her.

Speak more slowly and clearly, using shorter sentences and questions. Don't overload the person.

If you get stuck and can't get beyond the barrier, it may be that one of your colleagues may be better at communicating with that specific customer. People have different ears for language and accents, so someone else might be able to help the customer more effectively. If you think that might work, involve someone else in the situation.

See Also: 7. When You Need to Explain a Company Policy or Procedure

11. When the Customer Has Been "Buck-Passed"

THE SITUATION

Customers who have talked to three or four people and have not had any success getting help get angry and frustrated, because they feel employees are passing the buck. Unfortunately, they may aim their aggression at you, even though you don't have control over what other employees have done. What do you do?

TECHNIQUES USED

- Empathy Statements (1)
- Finding Agreement Points (2)
- Voice Tone—Emphatic (3)
- Assurances of Effort (4)

DIALOGUE

In this example, which could occur in person or on the phone, the customer is very upset because he has contacted or visited four government employees in three departments, only to find that none of them was the right person. What's worse is that each employee has referred him to the wrong person.

Customer: Someone in the Waterworks department sent me here and told me you could help me get my water reconnected and my account fixed, and I'm telling you, this better be the last stop I have to make, because I've been sent pillar to post and [starts going on and on].

Employee: I agree that this should never happen. (2) You shouldn't have to be spending all this time finding the right person to talk to and I can understand how frustrated you must be. (1)

Customer: Yeah, well, so can you help me?

Employee: Yes, I can. (3) Here's what I can do for you. (3) I'm not sure I can do everything you need, but what I *can* do is contact anyone else who needs to be involved and get things moving before you leave this office. That's what I'm going to do my best to accomplish. I will help you get this done. (4)

EXPLANATIONS

The employee responses can be used in situations where the employee knows that he or she can actually solve the customer's problem. They can also be used if the employee feels that he or she cannot solve the entire problem. What's key here is that the employee is making a commitment to the customer to get things moving *now*. Notice the employee's use of empathy up front (1) and the strong agreement sentence in (2). Also pay attention to the use of an emphatic tone of voice (3). Saying, "Yes, I can help you" in a strong voice that promises commitment is going to be much more effective than a flat or indifferent tone of voice.

HINTS

Never make commitments that you may not be able to keep.

In a buck-passing situation where you aren't the right person to help the customer, make the effort to find out who the customer needs to see. A lot of times buck-passing occurs because employees simply don't want to take the time to get an answer for the customer.

See Also: 9. When the Customer Has Been Through Voicemail Hell, 20. When YOu Don't Have the Answer, 23. When You Need to Route a Custome rPhone Call

12. When a Customer Needs to Follow a Sequence of Actions

THE SITUATION

There are some situations where a customer needs to follow a sequence of steps or actions in order to get something accomplished. For example, purchasing a house involves a series of steps, which would include selling the current house, finding a new house, engaging a lawyer, and arranging for a mortgage. Customers don't always know the sequence that is most advantageous. One role you can play is to help them navigate the sequence of steps. Here's how.

TECHNIQUES USED

- Empathy Statements (1)
- Assurances of Results (2)
- Providing Explanations (3)
- Providing a Customer Takeaway (4)

DIALOGUE

In this example, the customer is a first-time house-buyer working with a real estate agent for the first time.

Customer: Sheesh, I didn't know there was so much red tape and rigmarole involved with buying a house. It's a pretty scary, involved process.

Employee: It does seem overwhelming if you haven't gone through it before (1). I can help you get this organized, and I can tell you that it's almost always easier than it sounds, and we'll get through this (2)

Here's what I'm going to do. I have some printed information that will explain all the steps. Let's go over that material: I'll go through it step by step and you can ask questions. (3) [The employee brings out the printed material and goes through it with the customer, answering the questions.] (4)

EXPLANATIONS

Once again we see that the first step is to use an empathy statement. (1) In this case, the employee does this to help the customer understand that feeling overwhelmed is a "normal" reaction. She then emphasizes that the process is easier than it looks and it will all work out. (3)

Finally, she provides a customer takeaway that maps out the steps the customer needs to follow *and* covers each of the steps in a face-to-face conversation.

If there is no printed takeaway, the employee can make some simple notes by hand to summarize the conversation so the customer can take those notes with him and use them as a guide.

HINTS

It's useful to make notes to give to the customer even if there is printed material. At least mark the important points with a highlighter.

Takeaways should be simple and clear. They are best used as summaries of the face-to-face interactions between customer and employee.

Do not assume that your customer will understand or even read any written material you provide. You need to walk customers through the materials.

See Also: 7. When You Need to Explain a Company Policy or Procedure

13. When the Customer Insults Your Competence

THE SITUATION

Angry or frustrated customers sometimes vent or aim their anger about the situation at the most available person. That target could be you. One of the common attacks or insults has to do with the employee's competence or intelligence. How you handle this kind of situation means the difference between turning the situation into something positive and constructive and creating major hassles and upset for everyone. Here's how to deal with these insults.

TECHNIQUES USED

- Allow Venting (1)
- Empathy Statements (2)
- Not Taking the Bait (3)
- Refocus (4)

DIALOGUE

In this dialogue the customer is upset and chooses to make comments about the employee's competence and intelligence.

Customer: What the hell is wrong with you? Are you too stupid to understand what I'm trying to tell you? Or is it you just don't give a damn?

Employee: I can see you are concerned and I'd like to help. (1, 2, 3)

Customer: Damn right! I'm fed up having to deal with idiots like you.

Employee: I'd like to try to help you, but I need to ask a few questions. Let's see what we can do to get you what you need. (4)

EXPLANATIONS

The most important part of this example involves what the employee does *not* do. Although the insults are offensive, the employee realizes that if she reacts to them, the discussion will worsen into a flat-out argument, which won't help the customer and doesn't benefit the employee. So, she does not take the bait. (3) She focuses on showing the customer she understands he is upset using empathy (2) and also gives the customer some leeway to vent his frustration. (1)

After the customer has vented and not succeeded in getting the employee to jump at the bait, the employee tries to move the conversation away from the customer's anger and back to the reason why the customer contacted her. This refocusing (4) is intended to get back to the primary concern, issue, or problem.

HINTS

To help you not react to insults, keep in mind that the customer is, in effect, a stranger and should not be allowed to control your emotional reactions. And remember: you don't *have* to react with anger.

Keep in mind that if you end up in an argument, you are going to lose, since you don't have the freedom to unload on a customer, without running the risk of censure from your company.

It may not seem fair that you can't strike back—and it's not. If you take the bait, you end up suffering the consequences, in terms of stress, time, energy, and your reputation.

See Also: 25. When a Customer Threatens to Go over Your Head, 34. When a Customer Makes a Racist Remark

14. When a Customer Won't Stop Talking on the Phone

THE SITUATION

Sometimes customers will phone for help with a problem but are upset and do not allow you to respond to their concerns or even to help them. In this example, we'll try to get the customer to stop talking long enough so we can begin the helping process.

TECHNIQUES USED

- Telephone Silence (1)
- Empathy Statements (2)
- Assurances of Effort (3)
- Refocus (4)
- Offering Choices/Empowering (5)

DIALOGUE

The customer wants some help with an issue and has been talking on the phone with an employee almost continuously for two or three minutes.

Customer: … What kind of organization are you running here? I expect to get answers to my questions immediately, and when I call you just give me the runaround …. [continues to talk].

Employee: [says nothing—no uh-huhs, nothing at all] (1)

Customer: And another thing …. [continues for a time]. … Hello, are you there?

Employee: Yes, I'm here. It sounds like you are pretty upset (2), and I'm going to help you right now (3). I need to get a bit more information from you so I can help, so is it OK if I ask you a few questions? (4, 5)

Customer: Well, OK.

Employee: I only have a few questions. First, can you give me your account number?

EXPLANATIONS

You can't help someone unless you get the information you need, and you can't get that if the person is talking *at* you or rambling all over the place. In this example, the employee simply stops responding completely (1) until the customer is no longer sure if the employee is still there. (This works only on the phone.) When the person stops his constant stream of talk to ask whether the employee is there, it creates an opening for the employee to move the conversation back to whatever the customer has called about.

Note that the employee also wants to show the customer that his concerns and feelings are important (by using an empathy statement) (2) and to assure the customer that help will be offered immediately (3). He then refocuses (4) the conversation back to exploring the actual problem. This is done by asking permission or giving the person a choice. (5)

HINTS

- Keep using a calm tone of voice.
- Don't continually try to interrupt the customer, because that tends to cause him or her to start over or redouble the talk.
- Refrain from any signs of impatience, like sighing.

See Also: 17. When a Customer Won't Stop Talking and Is Getting Abusive on the Phone #1, 18. When a Customer Won't Stop Talking and Is Getting Abusive on the Phone #2

15. When the Customer Swears or Yells #1

THE SITUATION

While most customers are able to control their behavior to keep it within acceptable bounds, some customers, when they are angry, may swear and yell, or otherwise "act out". Obviously this is an extremely upsetting situation for most employees, and it also interferes with the employee's ability to do his or her job. It's hard to help someone who is yelling at you, and not paying any attention to what you are saying. In situations like this, your first goal is NOT to try to address the specifics of the customer's problem, but to use techniques to halt the inappropriate behavior. We are going to be using some advanced techniques to stop the customer's ranting, and get the customer to listen to, and respond to our efforts to help.

TECHNIQUES USED

- Some People Think That (Neutral Mode) (1)
- Finding Agreement Points (2)
- Empathy Statements (3)
- Assurances of Effort (4)

DIALOGUE

In this situation the customer is upset because he received a parking ticket that he feels is unwarranted. He visits the town clerk (which is where tickets are paid), and starts to yell and swear at the clerk at the counter.

Customer: What the [bleep] is going on here. One of your stupid meter maids gave me a ticket for parking near a hydrant and I wasn't within ten feet of the goddamn thing. I'm not paying this thing, and I want you to cancel the [bleep] thing *now*. [customer appears to be starting a long rant without stopping]

Employee: Some people feel that their tickets aren't deserved. (1)

Customer: Darn right. I'm one of them. I'm fed up.

Employee: I agree. You don't feel your ticket is deserved. (2)

Customer: So, what are you going to do about it?

Employee: Obviously you are upset about this. (3) You may not be aware that we have a way for you to appeal the ticket if you like.

Customer: Yeah? How?

Employee: I'll do my best to explain your options, so you won't be liable for an infraction you didn't commit. (4)

Customer: OK.

EXPLANATIONS

When the customer starts raising his voice, and using swear words the employee realizes that until the customer calms down and begins to listen to the employee, nothing at all can be accomplished. So, he uses "some people think... or neutral mode" to try to break into the conversation. The reason this technique works (when it does), is that it's an unexpected response that the customer doesn't have a ready made answer for. Unexpected responses tend to derail rants. Notice also that the neutral mode response is short. That's because an angry customer isn't going to "hear" a long response.

The customer responds by indicating he is "one of them". But what's important is the customer has become more attentive and is in the process of stopping the rant. The employee responds with an agreement point in (2). Notice that the employee isn't agreeing or disagreeing with whether the ticket is warranted or not, but is simply agreeing to the fact that the customer feels unfairly treated. Again, it's a short response.

The customer, while not happy, now behaves in a more constructive and acceptable way, which signals the employee that he can move the conversation to what the customer can do to dispute the ticket. First, the employee uses an empathy statement (3), and follows up with assuring the customer that he will make an effort to help. (4)

HINTS

When you act and speak as if you and the angry customer are on the same side, there's a tendency for angry customers to calm down, and stop yelling at you, since they don't see you as much as an "enemy".

Remember, with angry customers, you can't address their specific concern (in this case the ticket) until such time as the customer is calm enough to listen, and behave constructively to help solve his own problem.

With angry customers, look to engineer agreement. Look for things the customer says that you can agree with that will not put you in an awkward situation. Finding agreement points is such a powerful technique that it is often used by hostage negotiators.

See Also: 13. When the Customer Insults Your Competence, 16. When the Customer Swears or Yells in Person #2

THE SITUATION

In the previous chapter you saw one way of dealing with an extremely angry customer. It showed the importance of derailing customer rants, or inappropriate behavior. In this alternate example, you'll see how other techniques can be used for this purpose. We'll use the same situation as in the last chapter.

TECHNIQUES USED
- Distraction (1)
- Empathy Statements (2)
- Finding Agreement Points (3)
- Refocus (4)

DIALOGUE

As in the previous chapter, the customer is upset because he received a parking ticket that he feels is unwarranted. He visits the town clerk (which is where tickets are paid), and starts to yell and swear at the clerk at the counter.

Customer: What the [bleep] is going on here. One of your stupid meter maids gave me a ticket for parking near a hydrant and I wasn't within ten feet of the goddamn thing. I'm not paying this thing, and I want you to cancel the [bleep] thing *now*. I have children to take care of and a job where I don't get paid if I'm not there, so don't waste my time here…[customer appears to be starting a long rant without stopping]

Employee: How many children do you have. (1)

Customer: Well, three. What does that have to do with my [bleep ticket]?

Employee: I know it's a challenge enough to have to take care of children and go to a job everyday. (2)

Customer: Damn right it is.

Employee: Yes. It is. (3) Let's go back to the ticket, to see what we can do to provide you with an avenue to appeal. (4)

Customer: OK.

EXPLANATIONS

In this situation the employee uses Distraction—specifically a technique called "topic grab" (1). It is used to try to derail an angry customer by providing an unexpected response. In this situation, the employee "grabs" the reference to the customer's concerns about childcare, and asks the customer how many children he has. When the customer responds with a specific and short response, control of the conversation returns to the employee.

The employee responds with an empathy statement (2), followed by finding an agreement point. (3) Notice the artistry involved in creating a point of agreement. In (2) the employee offers an empathy statement, which the customer agrees with. In (3), the employee reaffirms the agreement, creating a sense that the customer and employee are on the same side.

Finally, the employee makes the transition from dealing with the customer's angry feelings, to dealing with the specific issue of the ticket and what the customer can do. This is done with a refocus statement. (4)

HINTS

The topic grab must be based on something the customer has said. You can't choose something at random, but must use something the customer has referred to that really has no connection to the customer's problem. Your topic grab question or statement must be short.

If the customer refuses to answer your topic grab, and responds with something like "It's none of your business," then you simply agree with *that* response "You're right, it really isn't. Let's see what we can do with the ticket." If the customer responds, and then stops to let you speak, the technique has done its job. Then you use the opening to refocus.

See Also: 15. When the Customer Swears or Yells in person #1, 17. When a Customer Won't Stop Talking and Is Getting Abusive on the Phone #1

17. When a Customer Won't Stop Talking and Is Getting Abusive on the Phone #1

THE SITUATION

Generally, people tend to be somewhat more aggressive on the phone than when talking in person. Sometimes a customer calls and begins an angry "rant," which includes insults, swearing, or other abusive behavior. It's best to try to derail the rant gently. But if the main technique in the previous situation (telephone silence) doesn't work, a firmer approach is needed. In this example, you want to stop the person so you can help and send the message that you will help but not unless the person stops swearing or otherwise ceases the offending behaviors.

TECHNIQUES USED

- Empathy Statements (1)
- Setting Limits (2)
- Offering Choices/Empowering (3)
- Assurances of Effort (4)
- Broken Record (5)

DIALOGUE

The customer wants some help with an issue and has been talking with the employee on the phone almost continuously for two or three minutes. In the last minute or two, the customer has started swearing and calling the employee names. In the example below, you'll see how to set limits on the caller's behavior to try to encourage him or her to stop the negative talk that is offensive to you and interferes with your ability to help.

Customer: What are you, a ******** idiot? I'm fed up with you people, and I'm fed up with you. You don't seem to know your *** from a hole in the ground.

Employee: Sir, I understand you are upset (1), but if you continue to yell and swear, I'll have to end the conversation. (2) It's up to you whether you would like to continue. (3)

Customer: I'd like you to get my damned check. Is that too much to ask?

Employee: I'll certainly try to help you with this (4), but I need your promise that you won't yell or swear at me. (5) Is that OK? (3)

Customer: Yeah, OK [reluctant]. Let's continue.

Employee: OK, good. I need to ask a few questions.

EXPLANATIONS

Notice that the employee began her response with an empathy statement (1) to soften the impact of setting limits later. She sets some limits that are specific and clear, sending the message that if the customer swears or yells, she will terminate the phone call. (2) It's important when setting limits to be as specific as possible and avoid general comments like "If you don't calm down…" or "If you aren't prepared to be civil …." Describe the specific problematic behaviors.

Pay special attention to the statement used in the limit setting—"It's up to you whether you would like to continue." We want to send the message that the customer is in control of whether the conversation continues and that the employee won't be punishing the customer or doing something *to* him or her. You want it to be clear that it is the customer's choice as to whether the conversation continues.

You can also see the use of several other techniques here. The employee uses reassurance (4) that she will indeed help, provided the customer stops yelling and swearing, and she completes the limit-setting process by using the broken record technique (5) to encourage the customer to make a specific commitment to stop the destructive behavior. She follows the repetition with a question—"Is that OK?" She uses this question to reinforce the idea that she is interested in the agreement of the customer and that they can work together.

In this case, setting limits works. But there are two other possibilities to consider. The first is that the customer continues to yell and swear. The second is that the customer agrees to stop, but then steps over the agreed-upon limits. We'll look at these in the next two situations.

HINTS

Setting limits isn't threatening or warning. Use a matter-of-fact voice because you are simply stating a fact. Use the same voice and tone you would use to say, "If you go out in the rain without an umbrella, you are going to get wet."

Within reason, you can draw your own lines regarding what is acceptable and unacceptable customer behavior, subject to the expectations of your employer. It is useful to allow some wiggle room for customers, because, on occasion, brief unpleasant outbursts will cease on their own and you can get on to helping the customer.

See Also: 14. When a Customer Won't Stop Talking on the Phone, 18. When a Customer Won't Stop Talking and Is Getting Abusive on the Phone #2

18. When a Customer Won't Stop Talking and Is Getting Abusive on the Phone #2

THE SITUATION

In the last chapter you saw an example of how setting limits can encourage a customer to stop negative behavior. But what happens if it doesn't work? In this example, we'll illustrate how to complete the limit-setting and limit-enforcing process. We'll simply extend the dialogue from the previous chapter.

TECHNIQUES USED

- Empathy Statements (1)
- Setting Limits (2)
- Offering Choices/Empowering (3)
- Setting Limits (4)

DIALOGUE

In this dialogue, the employee informs a customer of some behavior limits and the customer immediately steps past those limits.

Customer: What are you, an ******** idiot? I'm fed up with you people, and I'm fed up with you. You don't seem to know your *** from a hole in the ground.

Employee: Sir, I understand you are upset (1), but if you continue to yell and swear, I'll have to end the conversation. (2) It's up to you whether you would like to continue. (3)

Customer: I'd like you to get my damned check. Is that too much to ask, you stupid !x#!!* bleep?

Employee: I'm going to end this call. You are welcome to call back at some other time. (4)

Customer: [continues to swear]

Employee: [gently hangs up the phone]

EXPLANATIONS

This dialogue is identical to the one in the previous chapter, until the point where the customer ignores the limits and continues to swear and yell. The employee realizes that the customer is not likely to become less obnoxious right now and she can do little to help the customer until he stops the offending behavior. Having decided to end the call, she indicates her intention (4) and then says, "You are welcome to call back." She adds the latter invitation because she doesn't want to refuse service to the customer or be accused of hanging up. It's also an offer of a small bone to the customer.

It's generally not acceptable to simply hang up without a word. Hanging up without notice is also more likely to encourage the customer to call back, even angrier than before.

You can use the enforcing limits technique in a delayed fashion. Sometimes a customer will agree to abide by the limits you set, behave well for a minute or two, and then lose his or her temper and escalate into bad behavior. In that situation, you can repeat (broken record) the limit or begin the process of termination.

HINTS

Don't view hanging up or enforcing limits as punishment that's personal. All you are doing is trying to get control of the situation and encourage the person to stop the bad behavior *so you can help.*

Again, use a calm, matter-of-fact tone of voice.

Make sure you understand your organization's policy

about ending unpleasant customer interactions. Companies vary in terms of what they want employees to do in these situations.

Once you set a limit and indicate you are enforcing it (ending the conversation), the only thing that should keep you on the phone is a sincere, almost desperate apology. Ignore any grudging apologies and continue to end the conversation.

Don't set limits you aren't prepared and able to enforce. If you do, you lose all control and credibility.

Don't set limits and decide *not* to enforce them when required. Same reason as above.

See Also: 14. When a Customer Won't Stop Talking on the Phone, 17. When a Customer Won't Stop Talking and Is Getting Abusive on the Phone #1

19. When a Customer Has Been Waiting in a Line

THE SITUATION

In an ideal world, customers should be served immediately, without any waiting. But we don't work in an ideal world. Often the need for a customer to wait is a result of decisions made elsewhere in the organization, something you probably don't control. Is there a way of providing the best possible customer service when customers have to wait and reducing the possibility that the waiting customer will take out his or her frustration on you? Yes, there is.

TECHNIQUES USED
- Empathy Statements (1)
- Preemptive Strike (2)
- Assurances of Results (3)

DIALOGUE

In this example, the customer has been waiting to be served, either in a line or in a waiting area. This kind of situation occurs often in retail and in doctors' and dentists' offices, even when the customer has an appointment time. This dialogue highlights the importance of recognizing the customer's frustration before he or she has the chance to vent on the employee.

The employee notices that the line of customers waiting to be served has grown considerably over the last few minutes and that people in the line are showing signs of impatience—fidgeting, looking at their watches, sighing. This is what happens as the next person waiting approaches the service area.

Employee: I'm sorry you've had to wait (1) and I'm going to make sure you can finish up here as quickly as possible. (2, 3) What can I help you with?

EXPLANATION

This is called the preemptive strike: it works to defuse frustration and anger before the anger is expressed. It removes the incentive for the customer to complain and vent, since you have already acknowledged the customer's frustration. It paves the way for fast service.

You can add to this by providing an explanation of the reason for the delay, if you deem it helpful to the customer. For example, "I'm sorry you've had to wait, but the doctor had to deal with an emergency and is running late."

It's absolutely essential to the success of this technique that you speak first, before the customer has a chance to launch into a complaint. This helps you control the interaction and shortens the time needed, since you receive less lengthy complaints about delays.

HINTS

Speaking first allows you to gain control of the interaction and cuts down the amount of venting a customer may feel like doing about having to wait.

When things are behind schedule, consider making an announcement to the entire group of customers waiting and inform them of the approximate length of their wait.

See Also: 3. When a Customer Jumps Ahead in a Line of Waiting Customers, 5. When a Customer Interrupts a Discussion Between the Employee and Another Customer

20. When You Don't Have the Answer

THE SITUATION

It's almost impossible to have all of the answers to all possible questions customers may throw at you. When a customer asks you a question and you are unsure of the answer or simply don't know, you have two options—handle it the right way or the wrong way. The wrong way is to fake it, out of embarrassment, in the belief that the customer will think you stupid if you admit you don't know. The right way is to tell the customer you don't know, *but* to make a commitment to the customer to find out, either by researching and getting back to him or her or referring the customer to someone who will know.

If you fake it, you will find customers who will expose your ignorance for you. That's not a good feeling—and it's also bad business.

TECHNIQUES USED

- Acknowledge Customer's Needs (1)
- Offering Choices/Empowering (2)
- Referral to Third Party (3)
- Arranging Follow-Up (4)
- Suggest an Alternative to Waiting (5)

DIALOGUE

In this dialogue you will see several techniques strung together to address the situation where an employee does not have the answer to a customer's question. First, the employee tries to find the answer; then, when that does not succeed, the employee refers to a third party who does know the answer.

Customer: I'm looking at these DVD players, and I can't figure out why the prices are so different. Could you explain the differences between them?

Employee: I can see that you really need the right information and I want to make sure I don't give you inaccurate information. (1) Let me see if I can find the brochures so we can figure this out. It might take a minute or two. Is that OK? (2)

Customer: Sure, no problem.

Employee: If you want to browse some of the other items, I can look for the answers and get back to you when I've got something. (5)

Customer: That would be great.

The employee can't find the material and moves to plan B.

Employee: I think the best thing is for me to find John, who is really the DVD expert here. If anyone can help, it would be him. (3) If you have the time, I can do that now, or I can get back to you, or whatever works for you. (2)

Customer: I really can't wait right now, because I have a few other things to do. If I come back in 20 minutes, can I speak to John?

Employee: Yes, that would work well, and then you don't have to wait. I'll tell John to expect you, so just ask for him when you come in. (4)

EXPLANATIONS

The employee responds to the customer by acknowledging that the question is important to the customer, showing his concern for the customer's needs. (1) Before he leaves to find the information, he explains what he is doing and asks the customer if it's OK (2), an example of offering choices and empowering the customer.

In (5) the employee makes a suggestion—that rather than standing around waiting, the customer might prefer to browse some of the other items. Not only is this exceedingly considerate, but it's also a good way to encourage the customer to consider purchasing other items as well.

Unfortunately, the search for the brochures fails and the employee refers the customer to a third party (3). Note that the employee makes a special effort to describe John as the expert, which reassures the customer that the information he will eventually get from John will be accurate and useful and, best of all, worth waiting for. The employee also, once again, offers some choices by saying, "If you have the time, I can do that now…"

When the customer indicates he can't wait, the employee arranges for a follow-up (4).

There are some central themes here. We want to convey to the customer that we treat his or her need for information seriously and will do everything we can to provide that information, while inconveniencing him or her as little as possible. Throughout this dialogue, there's a sense that the employee is flexible and desires to go the extra mile. This turns a potentially embarrassing situation (lack of knowledge about merchandise) into a positive, an opportunity to demonstrate superior customer service skills and attitude.

HINTS

A customer who is waiting and doing nothing is a customer who will become annoyed and/or leave. Reduce waits as much as possible and offer something for the customer to do during waits (e.g., have coffee, browse other items, return in 10 minutes).

When referring to a third party, make absolutely sure the third party has the answers before making the referral. The best way to do that is to ask the third party before completing the handoff. The third party you refer to should be the last party the customer needs to talk with.

Keep the customer informed. Never walk away without explaining. Never say something like "Hold on a sec" and then walk off.

See Also: 21. When Nobody Handy Has the Answer, 24. When You Lack the Authority to ...

21. When Nobody Handy Has the Answer

THE SITUATION

Customers sometimes ask questions that nobody available can answer with confidence and authority. Such questions might be about a product's features or about a particular policy or procedure that has been developed in another part of the organization, and the customer service staff hasn't heard about it. If you don't know an answer and those around you don't know the answer, the question is still important to the customer. So, in the spirit of customer service, you still have an obligation to hunt down the answer.

TECHNIQUES USED

- Acknowledge Customer's Needs (1)
- Assurances of Effort (2)
- Offering Choices/Empowering (3)
- Arranging Follow-Up (4)
- Completing Follow-Up (5)

DIALOGUE

In this example, the customer asks for clarification of a particular policy about which the employee has not been informed. We join the dialogue at a point where the employee has concluded that he doesn't know the answer and neither do his colleagues and his immediate manager.

Employee: I can see that you feel it's important to have your question answered (1) and I'm going to do my best to get you an answer. (2) It will probably take me a day or two to find out and, when I do, I'd like to get back to you. What's the most convenient way to contact you with the answer? (3)

Customer: How about if I leave you my phone number and you can call and leave me a message?

Employee: I can do that. If you give me your number, I'll get back to you within 48 hours, one way or the other, so you won't be waiting and wondering. Does that work for you? (3, 4)

Customer: OK. I'll look forward to your call.

The employee then hunts down the answer. Regardless of whether he finds a definitive answer or not, he must respond within the 48 hours. If he has the answer, he phones to provide it. If he can't find the answer within the time period, then he phones as follows.

Employee: Mr. Jones, I wanted to get back to you about your inquiry. I haven't been able to get an answer for you, but I can refer you to someone who might know or you can call me to let me know if you want me to keep trying. (5, 3)

EXPLANATIONS

As with the dialogue in the previous situation, the employee makes sure to acknowledge that the question is important to the customer and to make sure the customer feels he has some choice and control. (1, 2) Then the employee arranges to go the extra mile by committing *personally* to follow up by trying to find the answer (3). The employee confirms the details of the follow-up and a time line/deadline by which he promises to contact the customer, whether he finds the answer or not. (4) Finally, you can see the actual follow-up process. (5)

What's important here is that the employee makes a personal commitment to help and the employee keeps that commitment and informs the customer.

HINTS

Never make a commitment to follow up that you may not be able to keep.

Keep your commitments each and every time. No excuses.

See Also: 20. When You Don't Have the Answer, 24. When You Lack the Authority to …

22. When You Need to Place a Caller on Hold

THE SITUATION

If you deal with any significant number of phone calls from customers, you will be in situations where you need to place a caller on hold. While nobody likes to be put on hold, the good news is that most callers are used to it, since it's become the norm. They are less likely to be annoyed if you handle the process professionally.

TECHNIQUES USED

- Explain Reasoning or Actions (1)
- Offering Choices/Empowering (2)
- Finishing Off/Following Up (3)
- Apologize (4)

DIALOGUE

In this situation the caller wishes to talk with the general manager of the company, who is currently on the phone with someone else, but is expected to be available shortly.

Employee: Mr. James is on the phone with another customer right now, but should be available in a few minutes. (1)

Customer: I'll wait. I need to speak with him as soon as possible.

Employee: OK, I can put you on hold and transfer you when he's available or we can call you back as soon as he's free. Did you still want to hold? (2)

Customer: Yes. I'll hold.

Employee: OK. I'll keep an eye on the lines and transfer you as soon as possible. (1) [puts customer on hold]

About one minute later, the employee checks back with the customer.

Employee: Hello. Mr. James is still on the other line. Did you still want to hold? (2)

Customer: Yes.

Finally, when Mr. James becomes available, the employee informs the customer as follows.

Employee: Hi. Good news. Mr. James is free. I apologize for the wait (4) and I'm connecting you right away. (2, 3)

EXPLANATIONS

What are the most important aspects of the employee's behavior here?

First, the employee informs the caller and explains the situation (1), rather than simply saying, "He's unavailable" and hitting the hold button. There are two reasons for this. One is to show the customer that he is important enough to merit an explanation. The other is to give enough information to the caller so he can make a decision about whether he wishes to be put on hold, call back, or pursue some other possibility.

Second, the employee allows the caller to make the choice as to whether he will be put on hold or not. (2) It is never advisable to put a caller on hold without both explaining why and giving the caller the choice. It may not always be possible to inform and offer a choice, particularly in a very busy switchboard environment, but it's worth trying.

The third important element is the follow-up. (3) It's important to check back with callers on hold to acknowledge that you know they are still waiting and to inquire if they'd like to receive a call back instead of waiting on hold. Notice also that the final sentence is an example of "finishing up." Rather than simply connecting the caller, the employee creates a sense of closure by telling the caller that Mr. James is available and that the employee is connecting them.

HINTS

Keep in mind that someone waiting on hold tends to experience time differently. One minute of wait time on hold might feel like four or five minutes of wait time in person. That's one reason why it's important to break up the wait time, by following up as possible.

See Also: 9. When the Customer Has Been Through Voicemail Hell , 23. When You Need to Route a Customer Phone Call

THE SITUATION

Customers don't always know who they need to speak to or even the specific department they need to contact. When a customer calls and isn't clear about who to speak to, your job is to get enough information to route the phone call to the right place the first time, so the customer can be served quickly.

TECHNIQUES USED

- Offering Choices/Empowering (1)
- Probing Questions (2)
- Active Listening (3)

DIALOGUE

In this example, the customer is calling about some issue with her check, but the employee is not immediately clear on the specific issue and therefore the person or department that needs to be involved.

Customer: I need to speak to someone about my check.

Employee: I want to make sure I direct you to the right person the first time, so can I ask you a few questions? (1)

Customer: Sure.

Employee: OK, are you calling because there's a problem with your check? (2)

Customer: No, I'm just looking for information about how I can change my tax deductions.

Employee: So, you want to know what paperwork you need to complete to make sure the tax deducted is more accurate. Is that what you need? (3)

Customer: Yes, exactly.

Employee: Good. You need to speak to Jan in payroll. I can transfer your call or give you the number to phone direct, whatever is more convenient. What works best for you? (4)

EXPLANATIONS

The employee needs to get enough information to route the call to the correct person. To get that information, the employee uses probing questions (2). Notice that the employee asks permission to do this in order to demonstrate to the customer that she is important (1).

If necessary, the employee would ask a longer series of questions.

In (3) the employee uses reflective listening to verify or confirm that he and the customer are on the same wavelength and that he understands what the customer wants.

Once the employee is confident he has enough information to direct the call, he indicates the specific person that the caller needs to contact and offers two options—transferring her to Jan or giving her the direct phone number so she can phone Jan at her convenience (4).

HINTS

When transferring a call, it's always good to inform the party receiving the transfer about the nature of the caller's needs or problem.

It's worth spending a few more seconds finding out what the customer needs before directing the call. When you direct a customer to the right place the first time, everyone wins. The customer feels valued and impressed with your competence and your coworkers and other employees spend their time more productively.

See Also: 22. When You Need to Place a Caller on Hold, 11. When the Customer Has Been "Buck-Passed"

24. When You Lack the Authority to …

THE SITUATION

You have probably been in situations where a customer asks you to do something for which you do not have sufficient authority. It might be as simple as reversing a transaction at a cash register, processing a return, or making an exception to a company policy or procedure. Here's how to handle this kind of situation.

TECHNIQUES USED

- Finding Agreement Points (1)
- Offering Choices/Empowering (2)
- Referral to Supervisor (3)

DIALOGUE

The customer approaches the employee and requests that she make an exception to a long-standing rule. However, she lacks the authority to violate the rule.

Customer: I don't see why I can't do [the thing prohibited by the policy]. It seems pretty reasonable and I'm sure I'm not the first to ask.

Employee: It does sound reasonable, (1) but I don't have the authority to say yes or no. The person who can approve that is the departmental manager, Mr. Smith. Do you want me to see if Mr. Smith is available? (2)

Customer: Sure.

Employee: OK. It will take a minute or two. [goes off to arrange the referral]

Employee: [returns to customer] Mr. Smith is available. To save you some time, I've explained to him what you are asking, so you won't have to repeat it, and I'm sure he'll help if he can. (3)

EXPLANATIONS

In this example, you see the employee actively trying to find agreement points (1). By agreeing with the customer that the request is reasonable, the employee helps the customer perceive that both of them are "on the same side."

The main technique used here is "referral to supervisor." The employee kicks off the referral process by asking the customer if he wants to talk to the supervisor about this issue. (2) Providing this choice allows the customer to decide for himself whether he wants to spend the time to talk with the supervisor or simply let the issue drop.

At the end of the referral process, it's important to communicate with the supervisor so he or she is prepared to deal with the customer in an informed way and knows in advance of any possible problem situation.

HINTS

When you lack the authority to fulfill a request *and* you also know the request is completely unreasonable and will be refused, it is still a good idea to arrange for the customer to speak with the decision maker. Customers tend to act more favorably when their request is refused by someone higher up (a supervisor or a manager).

As with any referrals, it's important that you and the supervisor are on the same wavelength regarding when it is appropriate or not appropriate to make the referral.

See Also: 26. When a Customer Demands to Speak with Your Supervisor, 20. When You Don't Have the Answer

THE SITUATION

Angry customers may threaten to go over your head, demand to speak with your supervisor or manager, or even try to intimidate you by demanding to speak with the "person in charge." The angry customer may want to talk with someone higher up because he or she believes that person will be better able to solve his or her problem *or* because he or she may be trying to intimidate or scare you into giving in to his or her demands.

TECHNIQUES USED

- Empathy Statements (1)
- Offering Choices/Empowering (2)

DIALOGUE

The customer is upset because the employee can't or won't do what the customer is asking.

Customer: If I don't get what I want, I'm going to go to your manager and your president, and then we'll see who is right.

Employee: I know you are unhappy about [topic of conversation] (1). If you believe it's best to talk to my manager, I can certainly help with that. Do you want me to help you arrange to talk to her? (2)

There are two common customer responses to this. The first is to back off from the threat, having realized the employee won't be intimidated. The second is to take the employee's offer. If the customer backs off, the employee turns the discussion back to the issue. If the customer continues to demand to talk to "the boss," the employee makes the effort to help the customer discuss the issue with the manager. (See Referral to Third Party technique for details.)

EXPLANATIONS

Once again, we see the employee using an empathy statement (1) to show the customer that his feelings are understood and acknowledged.

In the second part of the response, the employee does not resist or try to convince the customer *not* to contact someone higher up, but instead offers to help the customer do so, using options/empowerment to do so (2). There are two reasons why the employee uses this technique. The obvious one is that the customer is within his rights to ask to speak with the manager and the employee is simply acknowledging that and helping the customer do this. The second is that if the customer is bluffing for effect or to intimidate, providing that option will often convince the customer to give up that line of attack, since the employee does not seem to be intimidated.

HINTS

Different organizations and managers have different rules about making arrangements for a customer to talk with a manager or senior official. Find out what they are before using these techniques.

Offering to help tells the customer you won't be intimidated by threats and won't be manipulated. When in doubt, offer help.

See Also: 26. When a Customer Demands to Speak with Your Supervisor, 28. When a Customer Threatens to Complain to the Press

26. When a Customer Demands to Speak with Your Supervisor

THE SITUATION

One of the most common requests a frustrated customer makes is to speak with your supervisor or manager. A customer who demands to speak with your supervisor may be trying to intimidate you or may have a concern he or she feels will be best handled at the level above you. Customers who ask for such access may not even be frustrated, but believe that dealing with someone with more power is a faster, more efficient way to get what they want.

TECHNIQUES USED

- Probing Questions (1)
- Assurances of Effort (2)
- Not Taking the Bait (3)
- Referral to Supervisor (4)

DIALOGUE

In this example, the customer asks to speak to the supervisor right off the bat.

Customer: I want to speak to your supervisor.

Employee: I'll be happy to help you talk to Mrs. Jones (2), who is my manager, but is there anything I can do? (1) It might save you some time.

Customer: [sullenly] No. I don't want to speak to you. I'm tired of speaking to people who don't know what they are doing.

Employee: OK. I'll check to see if she's free, but it would help if I could tell her what you'd like to speak to her about. (3, 1)

Customer: Just tell her I want to talk about the poor service here.

Customer: OK. It will just take a minute. If you want to take a seat, I'll be back in a minute or two.

[The employee goes to the supervisor's office.]

Employee: Mrs. Jones, I have a customer who is demanding to speak to you about "poor service." Are you free? (4)

Supervisor: Sure, I'll come out and bring him or her to my office. [The employee and the supervisor approach the customer.]

Supervisor: Hi, I'm Mrs. Jones. I understand you wanted to speak to me about some service issues. If you'd like to come with me, we can talk where we won't be interrupted [gestures to customer to follow]. (4)

EXPLANATIONS

Since the customer asks to see the supervisor right off the bat, the employee doesn't know why this request is being made. So her first approach is designed to identify the "why," and to determine if the employee can be of assistance. To do that she asks one or two probing questions (1), while at the same time assuring the customer that the employee will make the effort to connect the customer to the supervisor. (2)

The employee quickly understands that this customer isn't going to provide any additional information. Note that the employee refuses to take the bait (3) when the customer says: "I'm tired of speaking to people who don't know what they are doing." In essence she simply ignores this backhanded swipe.

The second and third parts of the conversation show the mechanics of the referral to the supervisor. (4) In the second part, the employee explains the situation very briefly to the supervisor. In the third part, the supervisor and employee go to the customer. What's important here is that the supervisor takes control over the interaction immediately: she introduces herself, rather than the employee doing the introductions. You can see that, as part of the introduction, the supervisor says, "I understand you wanted to speak to me about some service issues." Why? To show that the employee has told her why the customer wants to speak with her and she is ready to discuss the issue.

HINTS

As an employee, you should know when your supervisor considers it appropriate to refer a customer to him or her and when it is not. If you are not clear about what your supervisor expects, ask.

While you may want to offer your services to help, instead of referring the customer to your supervisor, it's important to do this in a nondefensive way. Don't appear to be trying to dissuade the customer from speaking to the supervisor.

See Also: 25. When a Customer Threatens to Go over Your Head, 27. When a Customer Demands to Speak to Your Supervisor, Who Isn't Available

27. When a Customer Demands to Speak with Your Supervisor, Who Isn't Available

THE SITUATION

Your supervisor may not be immediately available when a customer demands to speak with him or her. Or maybe your supervisor really dislikes talking with customers and has made it clear that he or she doesn't want to do so. You have several options for dealing with these situations, but we're going to focus on an alternative—referring the customer to one of your peers.

TECHNIQUES USED

- Referral to Third Party (1)
- Acknowledge Customer's Needs (2)
- Offering Choices/Empowering (3)

DIALOGUE

In this example, the customer is upset because the merchandise he purchased seems to be defective.

Customer: This is the second time this week that I've gotten stuck with defective merchandise from you, and I'm fed up. I want to speak to your supervisor, and I want to speak to him now.

Employee: I can see that you want this resolved right away. (2) My supervisor isn't available right now, and I don't want to delay you, so I have a suggestion. John Jackson is an expert in this product line; if anyone can help you with this, he's your guy. (1) I know he's available, so if you like I can arrange for you to speak with him right now. If that doesn't work out, we can set up a time for you to speak with the manager. How does that sound? (3)

Customer: OK. I'll try that.

The employee then goes off to explain the situation to John. He returns to the customer with John, who introduces himself, making sure to demonstrate to the customer that he and the first employee have made an effort to discuss the customer's complaint.

John: I think I understand your problem. Let's see if we can get it solved for you.

EXPLANATIONS

The core element of this interaction is how the employee offers the referral. (1) The employee introduces the possibility of talking to John by highlighting his expertise about the customer's specific problem. In other words, he explains why talking to John will address the customer's problem—the faulty product. In reality, John may not have any more knowledge than the first employee, but by presenting John as an expert (which he is), the employee increases the chances the customer will respond positively to the offer and the interaction with John.

Notice also that the employee acknowledges the customer's need to get this resolved quickly (2) and leaves the decision to the customer by offering choices. (3)

HINTS

Never lie to a customer. If, for example, John knew absolutely nothing about the product in question, but was presented as an expert, no good would come from the referral.

As with referring to a supervisor, both the referring employee and the "expert" need to have arranged this referral process beforehand.

See Also: 26. When a Customer Demands to Speak to Your Supervisor, 29. When a CustomerDemands to Speak to the "Person in Charge"

28. When a Customer Threatens to Complain to the Press

THE SITUATION

Occasionally, an angry or frustrated customer may threaten to "go to the press" about how he or she has been treated by you and your company. Sometimes this is simply an empty threat intended to pressure you into doing what the customer wants. In other situations, it may be a genuine reflection of how upset he or she is. Here's a way to handle this situation.

TECHNIQUES USED

- Not Taking the Bait (1)
- Broken Record (2)
- Offering Choices/Empowering (3)

DIALOGUE

The customer has been dealing with the organization for a long time about a specific issue. Despite the organization's best attempts to solve the problem, the customer rejects any compromise solution offered. In a phone call, the customer threatens to complain to the press.

Customer: I've been trying to solve this problem for three solid months and I'm absolutely fed up. I think you need to be exposed for what you are and, by golly, I'm going to do it unless you do what I'm asking. I'm going to contact [newspaper name] and tell them everything. Then we'll see who wins.

Employee: That's certainly your right. (1, 2, 3) We'd prefer to come to an agreement with you, and I can suggest you speak to our VP of Finance, but it's really up to you which path you want to take. (3) Do you want me to arrange a discussion with the VP? (3)

Customer: Don't waste my time. If I don't get what I want, I'm going to the newspaper.

Employee: As I said, that's completely up to you. (3) If that's the case, then I guess we don't have anything else to discuss.

EXPLANATIONS

There's a theme that runs through this example. At no point in the conversation does the employee come across as defensive or overly concerned about the prospect of the customer going to the press. This is an example of not taking the bait. (1) By treating the threat as nonthreatening, he removes the power of the threat. Notice also that, while suggesting a preference for resolving the problem with the customer, the employee is not trying to directly dissuade the customer from carrying out the threat. Not taking the bait sends the message that the threat isn't going to work, in effect calling the customer's bluff.

The employee actively recognizes that the customer has the right to contact the press and recognizes this as an option for the customer. He emphasizes this by using the broken record technique (2).

HINTS

While no company or employee wants to appear in a negative light in the press, there is no guarantee that the press will agree with a customer who thinks he is being mistreated. In other words, the threat more often than not is not going to cause any problem.

The key thing to keep in mind is that you cannot fight

head to head in a situation like this. Don't appear to be put off balance by the threat and don't try to convince the customer not to contact the press. That is much more likely to cause the customer to carry out the threat.

See Also: 25. When a Customer Threatens to Go over Your Head, 29. When Customer Demands to Speak to the "Person in Charge"

THE SITUATION

Customers who feel—(rightly or wrongly)—that they are not getting what they want or not being treated the way they want sometimes demand to speak to the "person in charge," usually someone at the top of the organization. This could be a CEO, a vice president, or someone of equivalent rank and status. Often that person is not "on premises" and is not easily accessible to customers. Before discussing the best way of dealing with this situation, it's good to know that some percentage of people making such demands are sincere in wanting to talk to the person in charge. Others, however, use the demand to pressure, intimidate, or manipulate employees in the hope that they would rather give in than have to deal with a complaint registered with the executive. So, how do you handle this kind of situation?

TECHNIQUES USED

- Empathy Statements (1)
- Offering Choices/Empowering (2)
- Explain Reasoning or Actions (3)
- Providing a Customer Takeaway (4)
- Closing Interactions Positively (5)

DIALOGUE

In this example, the customer is upset because her auto insurance company has offered her much lower compensation for damage to her vehicle than she wanted. After the employee informs her of the settlement offer, she becomes exceedingly angry and, after arguing her case unsuccess-

fully, starts demanding to talk with the president of the insurance company, who is actually located in another city.

Customer: I've been paying these ridiculous premiums for over 20 years, and this is just the third time I've ever made a claim, and you're trying to screw me. I'm through wasting my time with you underlings. I want to speak to the president and I want to speak to him now.

Employee: It's clear you're disappointed in the figures, Mrs. Jones, and I can understand you want to speak to someone you think might be able to help. (1)

Customer: Damn right! And you aren't going to help much. So, let me speak to the president.

Employee: That would be Maria Pollock, the president of Loveme Insurance. If you want to go that route, instead of something that might be faster and easier for you, I'd be glad to help you get in touch with her. Before I do that, do you want to consider other options first? (2)

Customer: No, I don't want any "options." I want this Maria Pollock person.

Employee: OK. That's up to you. Maria Pollock is located at the head office in Lubbock. (3) You have a few options that I can help you with. You can phone her office, send her a fax, or write a letter outlining your concerns. If you tell me what you'd prefer, I can give you the information. (2, 3)

Customer: I want to speak to her *now*, right *now*.

Employee: OK. I understand you want fast action. (1) I'm going to write the president's name and toll-free number down for you, along with your file/incident number and related information. [while talking, writes down information] That way you won't have to pay for long distance and you'll have the information you'll need when you speak to her office. [hands information to customer] (4)

Customer: Why can't you just call now and give me the phone?

Employee: I'm sure you would prefer to have some privacy for your conversation and be able to call at your convenience.

Customer: Well, OK.

Employee: If you decide you'd like additional help, please feel free to get in touch with me. And also if you'd let me know how it goes, I would appreciate that. Anything else we need to do right now? (5)

Customer: No, I guess not.

Employee: OK. I'm sorry we couldn't come to some agreement. Good luck! (5)

EXPLANATIONS

There is an important theme that runs through the employee's responses here—nondefensiveness. It's essential that the employee not appear to be threatened by the demand. The best way to send a message of nondefensiveness is to be helpful to the person making the demand.

The employee first responds with an empathy statement (1), showing that she understands where the customer is coming from. After the customer reiterates her desire to speak with the president, the employee explains where the president is located and suggests that there might be other options that would work better for the customer. The employee could have specified the options (e.g., contacting the local manager, lodging an appeal, etc.), but decided to hint at them so as not to appear defensive. Since the customer remained adamant, the employee shifted to helping the customer contact the president by explaining options and providing information (2, 3).

The employee used some other techniques, ranging from another empathy statement to providing a takeaway to help the customer contact the president. The employee ends the conversation by offering further help and closing the conversation on a positive and nondefensive note (5).

HINTS

While we can never know for sure, the odds that a customer will actually take the time to follow through on his or her demand are relatively small. Employees still need to take such a demand seriously.

You may know that when the customer contacts the president's office, the chances of actually speaking with the president might be quite small, at least at first. Or you may know that the president's office is simply going to kick the problem back down the hierarchy. It's best to allow the customer to discover that himself or herself, rather than to point it out at the time the demand is made. If you say something like "Well, the president is very busy and it may take weeks to get a response," you'll simply come across as defensive. Provide other options beneficial to the customer in a light-handed way, but don't try to discourage him or her from contacting the executive.

See Also: 25. When a Customer Threatens to Go over Your Head, 28. When a Customer Threatens to Complain to the Press

30. When a Customer Makes an Embarrassing Mistake

THE SITUATION

Customers aren't always right. In fact, sometimes customers can be embarrassingly wrong. It may be tempting, particularly with a rude or annoying customer who blames his or her mistake on you, to point out the stupid mistake and put the customer in his or her place. While this is a great and common desire or fantasy, it's poor customer service and bad business. So how do you handle a situation where it's pretty clear the customer has made a very embarrassing error?

TECHNIQUES USED
- Empathy Statements (1)
- Bonus Buyoff (2)
- Refocus (3)
- Providing Alternatives (4)
- Face-Saving Out (5)

DIALOGUE

This situation takes place in a chain motel lobby, where four or five patrons are awaiting service. The obviously tired customer next in line announces that he has a reservation. The employee checks and can find no record of the reservation for that date, but does find a reservation for the next weekend. Since the motel is full, the employee cannot provide a room. In this situation, the employee, while annoyed at the customer's aggressiveness, decides that there is nothing to be gained by embarrassing the customer, particularly in front of the other patrons.

Customer: What kind of dip [bleep] place is this? I made a reservation, and now what? You lose it and now what am I supposed to do?

Employee: I know this is frustrating and you've obviously been traveling all day and want to relax. (1) I'm showing that you do have a reservation for next weekend and I'm thinking that, one way or another, something has gone awry here. (5) Since we don't have any rooms available right now, let's see what we can do. (3)

Customer: Next weekend? What the hell are you talking about?

Employee: Let's not worry about what's gone wrong right now, but let's find you a place to stay. (3) We have another motel about a mile from here. I'll see if we can book you there. (4) Is that OK?

Customer: Well, OK. But I'm still not happy about this.

Employee: Tell you what, I'll see if I can get you a discount or an upgrade at the other motel. (2)

EXPLANATIONS

The employee's front-line response is to use an empathy statement (1) to indicate she understands the customer is tired and anxious to find a place to stay.

The most important part of this dialogue involves two techniques—refocusing and providing a face-saving out. You can see in the responses marked (3) that while the customer seems to want to complain and blame, the employee refocuses the conversation on what is really the issue, finding the customer a place to stay. Even with an angry customer who has made a mistake, the logic for doing so is compelling. The second technique, providing a face-saving out, is shown where the employee says, "Something has gone awry" rather than suggesting that the customer has confused the dates and thus caused his own misfortune. That's because it doesn't matter *who* made the mistake; even if the employee *knows* the error lies with the customer, there's no reason to point it out—especially since, when a customer feels embarrassed or humiliated, one response is to strike out in anger at the employee.

Once the employee refocuses on the real issue, she goes the extra mile to arrange a room elsewhere and even offers a discount as a form of bonus buyoff, even though it's the customer who made the mistake. (2)

HINTS

While it's tempting to force an annoying customer to acknowledge the error lies with him or her, there's no benefit in doing so. Embarrassed people often strike out. That means the interaction takes longer and can become more and more unpleasant. That's not good for the customer, for you, or the other customers who are waiting in line.

Another reason to avoid embarrassing a customer who has seemingly made an error is that you may not be absolutely sure the mistake lies only with the customer. It's better to stay away from the "blame game," because whether the customer is at fault or you are, you will lose.

See Also: 33. When a Customer Is Confused About What He or She Wants or Needs, 46. When a Customer Wants Information You Are Not Allowed to Give

31. When a Customer Withholds Information Due to Privacy Concerns

THE SITUATION

Some people are very protective of their personal information, even to the point where they may refuse to provide information to you that may be essential or helpful in determining the best way to provide assistance. For example, a person might call a doctor's office to make an appointment and not want to tell the receptionist the nature of the medical problem. We can all understand someone wanting to keep personal details limited to as few people as possible. Surprisingly, some people are so "private" that they may not want a retail store clerk to know what size of trousers they wear. How do you handle these situations professionally and without causing embarrassment?

TECHNIQUES USED

- Offering Choices/Empowering (1)
- Face-Saving Out (2)

DIALOGUE

A rather large man is browsing the suits in a mid-scale men's clothing store. He's looking at suits that are clearly not going to fit him. After greeting the customer and identifying that the customer wants to purchase a new suit, the employee continues.

Employee: Perhaps we should take some measurements so you won't waste time looking at suits that won't fit. Is that OK? (1)

Customer: [brusquely] *No.* Thank you, but no. I'd rather look.

Employee: That's fine. That may be a good idea, since if you find something you really love, but we don't have it in your size right now, we can probably order it for you. (2)

Customer: Yeah, that's right. I want to see what I like first.

Employee: If you'd like, I can show you some of our newest items. Or you can look around on your own and give me a shout if you would like some help. (1)

Customer: OK, I'll just let you know, then.

Employee: OK. [walks off to straighten the tie rack]

EXPLANATIONS

It may seem odd that this customer might not want the employee to know his size, particularly since someone is going to have to ring up his purchase (if he makes one) and will obviously see the information anyway. But it really doesn't matter, because good customer service dictates that we try to make the customer as comfortable as possible. That means accommodating individual quirks and eccentricities when possible.

This example is fairly straightforward. You can see that the employee offers choices to the customer (1) and gives him control of the interaction. Notice how the employee uses the "face-saving out" (2). When the customer says he wants to browse and he seems upset at the prospect of the employee taking measurements, the employee provides a plausible explanation for why browsing could be a good plan, in essence agreeing with the customer, rather than arguing that they should determine the customer's size right away. This technique is intended to avoid embarrassing the customer by any mention of his size.

HINTS

Whenever possible, try to accommodate the customer's desire for privacy. If you cannot do so, then make sure you explain why you need the information to assist the customer.

Stay alert to customer quirks and potential areas that may be embarrassing for the customer. Remember that a customer may be embarrassed by things that would not embarrass you and that it's your job to try your best to be sensitive to that fact and to make the customer comfortable.

See Also: 30. When a Customer Makes an Embarrassing Mistake, 59. When a Customer Asks Inappropriate Questions

32. When a Customer Threatens Bodily Harm or Property Damage

THE SITUATION

One of the most stressful situations in customer service occurs when a customer threatens bodily harm or property damage. Apart from the obvious sense of concern that an employee feels about his or her welfare, stress is magnified because of the uncertainty of the situation. When threats occur, questions flood in. Will the person actually carry through on the threat? What should you do? How can you stay safe?

There are many kinds and degrees of threat, which compounds the difficulty. Some threats are made from a distance, where the employee isn't in immediate danger. Some are general, some specific. Some are direct, some indirect. Since dealing with threats is complex and the consequences of making a wrong decision can be severe, in most situations, an employee should rely on the organization's policies and procedures for dealing with emergencies or threats and let law enforcement or security professionals make the tough decisions. They are trained for it. You are not.

When a customer utters a threat of any kind, the issue is no longer customer service, but safety, protection, security, and law enforcement. For this reason, detailed discussion and advice on dealing with most threats are beyond the scope of this book. However, we will look at a situation where the employee is not in immediate danger and a general threat has been made over the phone. We'll add some extra explanation and hints to this particular example that apply to other kinds of threat situations.

TECHNIQUES USED
- Use Customer's Name (1)
- Empathy Statements (2)
- Setting Limits (3)
- Contact Security/Authorities/Management (4)

DIALOGUE

A clearly upset customer calls and, during the phone call, makes a generalized threat.

Customer: I'm absolutely fed up with you people. I have a mind to come down there and show you can't mess with me. You know I can get you if I want.

Employee: Mr. Jones, (1) I understand that you're concerned and worried about [summarize issue]. (2) I will do the best I can to help you with this, but I can't do so if you talk in an aggressive way.

Customer: Maybe you'll be more helpful if I come down there with a crowbar.

Employee: Mr. Jones (1), if you continue to talk in a threatening way, I'll have to end this conversation. It's up to you whether you want to continue to talk right now. (3)

After the conversation ends, the employee then informs security, the authorities, and/or management, according to the organization's policies and procedures, in order to maximize safety and security. (4)

EXPLANATIONS

This situation involves an indirect threat, but in any threat situation it's important to remain calm, sound calm, and not overreact. That's why the employee's initial response involves using the customer's name (1) and an empathy statement (2). The interaction may not be doomed: the employee is still trying to work to resolve the problem or at least to get the customer to tone down the discussion. This is more appropriate when the threat is indirect and there is no obvious immediate danger.

The customer steps up the threat, making it more specific by mentioning the crowbar, at which point the employee decides that if the threats continue in any shape or form, the conversation must end. He sets a limit, which he will enforce if necessary. If the customer does not calm down or rescind the threat, it's absolutely essential that the employee report the threat to his manager, the authorities, and/or security. The most compelling reason to do so is to alert them to a possible problem so they can prepare to deal with it if it occurs.

If the employee succeeds in calming down the customer and the phone call or interaction is resolved calmly and constructively, whether the employee reports the incident or not is a judgment call. However, since uttering threats is illegal in most places and since a customer may make a habit of threatening employees, it's probably best to report threats even if the situation seems to have been resolved.

HINTS

Err on the side of safety and security. While many verbal threats are just words born of anger and frustration, you won't know which of the threats is serious and sincere.

Let the professionals decide. The police and security should have more experience in these situations and better training. That's why it's best that all threats be reported, at minimum to management.

If you feel you are in serious danger, contact the police, even if your company prefers you don't. Better to deal with an angry boss than become a violence statistic.

It is important that you remain calm in threat situations. When you react emotionally, you may be providing the threatening person with reinforcement (or reward) for making the threat. In a situation where you may feel endangered, the more emotional you get, the more unpredictable your behavior may be, and that behavior may startle or upset the person threatening you.

After any threat incident, you will want to make some notes about the situation, the context, the person making the threat, and so on to provide to management, security, or the police. For example, if the threat is made in person, you might want to note any information you might have about the person—physical description, characteristics, voice, etc. If on the phone, you might want to note the caller's number, the tone and kind of voice, and any background noises.

Your company or organization should have guidelines and procedures for these kinds of situations. Follow them unless you feel that doing so will result in immediate harm to you, your colleagues, or other bystanders. If your company does not have such guidelines, it should. Suggest that management develop them. In the absence of guidelines, talk to your manager so he or she and you are on the same wavelength about how these situations should be handled.

See Also: 36. When a Customer Refuses to Leave, 39. When a Customer Might Be Stealing

33. When a Customer Is Confused About What He or She Wants or Needs

THE SITUATION

In many customer service situations, the employee's role is to help the customer buy or obtain something, in a situation where the customer is fairly clear about what he or she wants. In other situations, the customer may not be clear about which product or service to buy, which person to speak with, or other matters. When a customer is confused, the employee needs to help the customer clarify his or her wants or needs.

TECHNIQUES USED

- Probing Questions (1)
- Empathy Statements (2)
- Active Listening (3)
- Expert Recommendations (4)
- Above and Beyond the Call of Duty (5)

DIALOGUE

In this example, which occurs in a government office, a customer is very unclear about the person to see or talk with or even what she wants. The customer has a problem, but has no idea how to use government services to solve that problem.

Customer: I'm a single mother and I need financial help to pay for my children's school.

Employee: OK. I'm not sure this is the office you need, so I'm going to ask you some questions so I can suggest who you need to speak with in order to get some help. OK?

Customer: Sure. I'm a little lost with all this.

Employee: Understandable. You're probably pretty worried about your kids and navigating the various government offices can be confusing. (2) First, let's start with who you've talked to so far. Is this your first government visit about this? (1)

Customer: Yes.

Employee: [asks questions about the age of the children, the income level of the customer, whether the father is paying support, etc., which the customer answers] (1)

Employee: All right. I think I understand. Let's see if I have this right. You have two children and your husband has left you and is refusing to pay support to help pay for school supplies. You're wondering what your options are. Is that right? (3)

Customer: Yes. I just need to get by this rough spot.

Employee: OK. We don't handle requests for temporary assistance in this office, but I can help. Here's what you need to do. You can apply for short-term assistance at the Department of Family Affairs on Green Street, which is right around the corner. (4) They can help you with that end. I'd also suggest that you contact the Child Support Enforcement Agency as soon as possible for advice. (4) It may turn out that there are ways to encourage your husband to pay for the school supplies, but you need to talk to the experts. They are also on Green Street. (4)

Customer: OK. Can you give me directions?

Employee: Yes, I'll do that. I'm also going to give you my card, so you'll have a specific person to talk to if you need more help on this. (5)

EXPLANATIONS

Most of this conversation consists of the employee using probing questions (1) to get enough information to provide expert advice to the customer. Clearly, to give proper advice, the employee must take the time to understand the customer's situation. Once the employee believes he has enough information to provide that advice, he checks out his understanding of what the customer has said, using active listening to summarize the customer's situation. (3) This is an essential step, because if the employee misunderstands, the customer may end up going to the wrong places, because the advice will not fit. Active listening provides an opportunity for the customer to correct the employee's understanding.

Then the employee offers expert recommendations. (4)

Pay special attention to the last sentence, where the employee offers his card so the customer will have a known point of contact. (5) This is something the employee is not required to do; it's above and beyond the regular call of duty. It's offered as a means of reassuring the customer that she can call a specific person if she gets lost in the bowels of the government system.

HINTS

Make sure you understand the customer's situation before handing out advice. It's easy to jump to conclusions and not listen effectively—and end up not helping at all.

If you do not have enough knowledge to provide expert advice, then don't. Either refer the person to somebody who is more expert or be honest and simply admit you don't know.

34. When a Customer Makes a Racist Remark

THE SITUATION

One of the most offensive things one person can say to another is to make a racist remark—a negative comment about the person's ancestry, culture, heritage, or skin color. It's unacceptable in any civil social situation and it's no less unacceptable during an employee-customer interaction. And let's not make the mistake of assuming that racist remarks are uttered only by those in the "dominant culture." No particular group has a monopoly. Racism is racism.

But how can you handle such a situation in a professional way that does not open you up to a long, drawn out argument?

TECHNIQUES USED

■ Setting Limits (1)

DIALOGUE

In this example, the customer makes a remark about the employee's skin color. In this example, we'll use the color green to refer to the employee's skin color.

Customer: Well, I guess I shouldn't expect you green people to have any brains at all. All of you are brought up in barns or something.

Employee: I'm willing to help you conduct your business with us, provided you don't make any further comments about my background. If you do make any further remarks like that, I'm going to end this conversation and ask you to leave. (1) It's up to you, but I need your agreement before we can continue. (1)

Customer: I have a right to my opinions. It's a free country.

Employee: It seems like you've made your choice, so I'm ending this conversation. If and when you are willing to talk without negative remarks, I'm willing to help. But right now, this conversation is over.

EXPLANATIONS

This is a volatile situation and there is no perfect solution. What you want to do is make it clear that the customer must meet a certain requirement—to stop making racist/negative comments—if the conversation is to continue. That's why the major technique involves setting and enforcing limits (1). In setting the limits, it's important to do so in as neutral and matter-of-fact tone as you can muster. The less you show emotional reactions, the less likely the situation will escalate.

Setting limits is a first step. The much harder part is enforcing the limits you set. If this conversation occurred on the phone, you could terminate the conversation, since that's something you have control over. If it occurs in person, let's say in your company's office, that's much tougher, since you do not have direct control over whether the unpleasant customer leaves or not. You can refuse to interact further, but that raises a question: What do I do if the person doesn't leave the area? The answer: it depends on your company policy and whether you have security personnel available to enforce the limits and the consequences you set. What's clear is that you should never take it upon yourself to try to remove such a person from the office. Situations like this can escalate to violence if not handled properly.

If the person refuses to leave, probably your best bet is to remove yourself from the vicinity. For example, if the person is in your office, you can get up and leave. If you can't do that and the person is interfering with business, then this may become a security or law enforcement issue.

If this occurred outside of the office, let's say on the premises of the customer, then you would leave, applying the consequences you mentioned in setting the limit.

HINTS

While you may be completely outraged by the remarks, keep in mind that your job is not to make the customer into a better human being. You will always lose if you engage in a long lecture about making racist remarks. Keep things short and simple. Don't argue.

When applying a consequence, like ending an interaction or asking the person to leave, you should always consider your own physical safety and the safety of those around you. There are times when the best path is to do nothing to get the person to leave. Try not to escalate and try not to back yourself into a corner, literally and figuratively. Safety first.

See Also: 35. When a Customer Makes a Sexist Remark, 37. When a Customer Accuses You of Racism

35. When a Customer Makes a Sexist Remark

THE SITUATION

While customers probably use sexist language less these days, employees still encounter sexist remarks much more frequently than many of us would think. Both men and women can be the victims of sexist comments, but women are more likely to be the targets. In this section we'll look at one way to deal with a somewhat indirect, demeaning, sexist remark.

TECHNIQUES USED

- Not Taking the Bait (1)
- Refocus (2)
- Pros and Cons (3)

DIALOGUE

The employee is a car mechanic who is highly qualified and expert at her job. The customer, unfamiliar with having a woman work on his car, expresses a lack of confidence in an obnoxious, sexist, and insulting way.

Customer: Look, I want someone to look at my car who knows what he's doing. Isn't there a man around?

Employee: If you are concerned about my experience, I've been a mechanic for over 10 years and I've had my license at least that long. Now, you mentioned a funny noise coming from the engine. Can you describe it for me? (1, 2)

Customer: I don't see how a woman can know anything about cars.

Employee: Well, the thing is that if you want your car fixed today, I'm the only person available. So it's up to you what you want to do. Do you want to discuss the problem with your car so we can get it done for you? (3)

Customer: OK, let's do it.

EXPLANATIONS

While the sexist remarks are exceedingly demeaning and insulting, notice that the employee refuses to be drawn into an argument about the ability of women to fix cars. She realizes that if the customer is sexist, it's not likely that arguing with him is going to change his mind. So, first she avoids the bait (1). She very briefly assures the customer that she is experienced and skilled, *but* almost in the same breath she refocuses (2) back to the customer's reason for being there—the problem with the car.

Unfortunately, the customer responds to the refocus with another sexist comment. The employee responds by providing incentive for the customer to put aside his prejudice (really a Pros and Cons technique) (3), by explaining that if he wants the car problem repaired today, she's the mechanic he will have to deal with.

Faced with this reality, the customer gives in.

HINTS

There is a difference between sexist remarks and behaviors and a legitimate desire to work with a man or a woman. For example, a man arranging a psychotherapy session may have a legitimate desire to work with another man (or a woman) because he feels more comfortable and his comfort may be essential to the success of psychotherapy, at least for him. His request to work with a man (or woman) isn't based on any prejudice about male or female competencies. However, when a request is phrased in terms that imply one gender or the other is inferior, then the request is sexist.

While sexist remarks may cause considerable anger, remember two things: you aren't going to change the other person and the person is a stranger whose opinions shouldn't be allowed to control your emotions. There's no point in arguing.

However, when a customer makes sexist remarks over and over and it's clear that his or her attitude is going to prevent you from doing your job to help, you can consider terminating the conversation or giving in and arranging for the customer to be served by someone else—of the preferred gender. It's a judgment call. You can also refer the individual to a supervisor.

See Also: 13. When the Customer Insults Your Competence, 34. When a Customer Makes a Racist Remark

36. When a Customer Refuses to Leave

THE SITUATION

While it is rare, you may find yourself in a situation where you have exhausted all constructive mechanisms of conversation and have decided to terminate the conversation with a customer. You politely ask the customer to leave, but he or she refuses. What do you do?

TECHNIQUES USED

- Setting Limits (1)
- Disengaging (2)
- Contact Security/Authorities/Management (3)

DIALOGUE

This situation occurs in the office of the employee. The customer is angry at not getting what he wants and has become abusive. The employee sets some limits, indicating that unless the customer ceases his abusive behavior, the employee will ask him to leave. The customer responds abusively.

Employee: I don't think we can continue this conversation, so I'm going to ask you to leave.

Customer: I told you I'm not leaving until I get what I want. I'd like to see you try to make me leave.

Employee: I'm not going to force you to leave, but I'm not going to continue with you. I'm going to leave.

Customer: Well, I'm not going anywhere.

Employee: Fine. If you are still here when we close our office in 20 minutes, we'll have to contact the authorities to escort you out of the building. I don't think anyone wants that.

Customer: I'm not moving.

Employee: [leaves the office and informs manager and/or security of the problem] (3)

EXPLANATIONS

The employee recognizes it isn't his job to remove the customer and chooses the path of least resistance. Since there is no immediate safety threat and the customer is not actively interfering with the business of others, the employee decides to let the customer sit in the office. Faced with refusal to leave, the employee sets forth the limits and consequences if the customer stays (1) and then disengages by leaving the office (2).

When the customer realizes he is sitting in an office by himself, without anyone to talk to, he may choose to leave on his own, understanding the whole process has become pointless. If he tries to stay beyond closing, then there is no choice but to contact security or the authorities to have him removed.

This situation is a potentially serious one that may impact safety and security, so it's important that the employee, upon exiting from the office, inform his supervisor or security immediately, so he or she can decide on the best course of action.

HINTS

In this example, the employee could have checked back with the customer after allowing him to sit by himself for five or 10 minutes. For example, "Mr. Smith, if you are willing to discuss your situation in a quiet manner, I'm willing to do that." Sometimes an angry customer will reconsider after having had a few minutes by himself or herself and either act more civilly or choose to leave.

There is no magic solution to this kind of situation that guarantees everyone wins. Keep safety and security firmly in mind and do not escalate or raise the stakes. Above all, don't take on the responsibilities of the police or security.

See Also: 32. When a Customer Threatens Bodily Harm or Property Damage, 39. When a Customer Might Be Stealing

37. When a Customer Accuses You of Racism

THE SITUATION

One of the most offensive verbal attacks a person can make on another is to accuse him or her of being racist. While these kinds of attacks don't happen that often, when they occur, self-control is essential for keeping the situation from becoming even uglier and more destructive. In this example, we assume that the employee has not done anything at all to justify the accusation.

TECHNIQUES USED

- Empathy Statements (1)
- Refocus (2)
- Referral to Supervisor (3)
- Not Taking the Bait (4)
- Offering Choices/Empowering (5)

DIALOGUE

In a government office, a person from a minority group (we'll call it the "green" group) is frustrated and angry because he is not being given what he asks for. He strikes out verbally at the employee.

Customer: If I wasn't green, you'd give me what I'm asking for. I think you are just prejudiced against green people.

Employee: It sounds like you are pretty frustrated. (1) I can explain how to appeal the decision, if that's what you want. (2, 4, 5)

Customer: What's the point? All of you people are the same. You don't like green people.

Employee: If you would like to talk to my supervisor about the decision, I can help you arrange that. Is that what you'd like to do? (3, 5)

Customer: Yeah, I guess so.

EXPLANATIONS

The most important thing to notice here is that the employee, while indirectly acknowledging the "racist accusation," doesn't focus on it, but continues to turn the conversation to the issue (whatever the customer came in to discuss). He responds calmly and refuses to get into or encourage an argument about the accusation of racism, in essence refusing to rise to the bait (4).

Notice that the employee uses an empathy statement (1) that acknowledges the customer's feelings of frustration, without directly acknowledging the racist accusation. The employee offers a suggestion or choice about explaining the appeal process (2, 3), which the customer refuses or ignores.

Sometimes a customer will accuse an employee of racism as a way to get attention or intimidate the employee into doing what he or she wants, even though the customer does not really believe the accusation. Responding positively and not getting pulled in can encourage such people to back off the accusation.

However, in this case, that doesn't happen. The customer repeats the accusation, this time suggesting that everyone discriminates against green people. Since this kind of accusation is something that the employee cannot ignore if the customer continues to bring it up, the employee decides this situation would best be handled by the supervisor. He offers the possibility of speaking with the supervisor (3) and leaves the decision up to the employee (5).

HINTS

Accusations of racism need to be taken more seriously than other kinds of accusations or insinuations, because the customer may decide his concerns (legitimate or not) should be aired in the media or to senior company staff. Generally, you should try to acknowledge any anger but without addressing the accusation directly, until such time as you believe the customer is serious. Then you need to address it more directly.

Self-control here is crucial. Your natural reaction may be to defend yourself, but that reaction usually fuels an argument. The accusation may be unfair and unjustified. However, you aren't going to change the accuser's mind when he or she is persistent. Arguing isn't likely to result in the accuser stopping the accusations. Arguing *will* cost time, and result in even more frustration.

See Also: 34. When a Customer Makes a Racist Remark, 35. When a Customer Makes a Sexist Remark

38. When a Customer Plays One Employee Off Another ("So-and-So Said")

THE SITUATION

On occasion you may come across a customer who plays one employee off another. There are two situations where a customer may do this. In one situation, a customer contacts one employee (a coworker of yours) and then contacts another employee (you) and receives information that is inconsistent. In that situation, a customer might say, "But I spoke to John (coworker), and he said that I could .... " In this situation, the customer is acting in good faith and is confused about the conflicting information he received.

In the second situation, the customer is not acting in good faith: he or she lies about getting different information from another employee and is hoping that you will bend the rules and buckle to the pressure of "what so-and-so said" to do what he or she wants. Customers will sometimes contact a number of employees, hoping to find someone who gives the answer the customer wants. You may recognize this as similar to what children sometimes do with their mothers and fathers.

The challenge is that it's hard to tell if a customer is playing off one employee against another as a way of manipulating or whether it's a good-faith effort to resolve conflicting information. How do you handle a situation where you don't know whether the customer is being honest about what another employee said, or whether the customer might be honestly mistaken?

TECHNIQUES USED

- Not Taking the Bait (1)
- Offering Choices/Empowering (2)
- Summarize the Conversation (3)

DIALOGUE

In this situation, the customer calls to try to get an employee to make an exception to a particular procedure. The employee cannot tell whether the caller is legitimately asking for clarification or trying to manipulate when he uses the "so-and-so said" phrasing. The employee informs the caller that he is unable to do what the customer asks.

Customer: Well, I don't see the problem. I spoke to John McGee yesterday and he said there wouldn't be a problem in getting this done.

Employee: I can't address what John McGee might have said to you, since I wasn't part of the conversation. Which leaves us a few options. You can get back in touch with John and continue the discussion with him or we can talk about your situation a bit more to see whether we can find some way to accommodate you that works for both of us. Which would you prefer? (2)

Customer: Well, John's hard to get in touch with, so maybe we can continue to talk about this, since I have you on the phone.

Employee: OK. Let's see if I understand your situation properly. You want to [fill in relevant information] and you would like us to make an exception because [fill in relevant information]. Is that right? (3)

EXPLANATIONS

When a customer starts the employee-versus-employee tactic, it creates a problem. If the employee deals directly with what the customer says as if it is true and accurate, the employee may end up manipulated. On the other hand, if the employee completely ignores what another employee might have said, that can result in inconsistencies or even conflict between employees. So, the employee's first response is to avoid taking the bait (1). The employee acknowledges that he heard what the customer said, but does so in a way that doesn't commit to further discussion about what the other employee might have said. At this point, there is little reason to go into any detail about what John said, unless John is involved in the discussion.

However, since the employee doesn't know what's happened, what's true, and what John really said, he provides the opportunity for the customer to go back to John to finish conducting his business. This sends the message that the employee is being flexible and helpful and leaves the decision with the customer (2).

If the caller is not quite telling the truth about what John said, then it's likely the caller will not want to go back to John. In effect, offering this choice is a way of calling the customer's bluff, if it is a bluff, without being obvious or offensive about it.

When the customer decides not to contact John, the employee returns the conversation to the issue at hand by summarizing the situation as he sees it (3). Apart from showing he is listening, summarizing addresses the possibility that the employee has missed something important about the situation that might have caused John to give conflicting information. It's a form of clarification, just in case.

HINTS

In a "so-and-so said" situation, you really can't comment on a conversation you were not a party to, no matter how much the customer wants to push you into it.

Remember that you simply don't know what John said or what information John used to draw his conclusions. Either avoid the bait or, involve John in the discussion.

Keep in mind that even if a customer is providing an honest recollection of what your colleague said, that recollection may be inaccurate, incomplete, or garbled.

See Also: 40. When a Customer is Playing to an Audience of Other Customers, 41. When a Customer Exhibits Passive-Aggressive Behavior

THE SITUATION

Strictly speaking, theft and shoplifting shouldn't be customer service issues, but it's not uncommon for an employee to have suspicions or be confronted by situations where a "customer" is stealing. What to do?

TECHNIQUES USED

■ Contact Security/Authorities/Management (1)

DIALOGUE

This situation is different from most, because what counts is not what you say to a suspected shoplifter, but what you do. In this situation, an employee observes someone stuffing an item into his pocket, apparently with the intent of stealing.

There should be no dialogue with the suspect. (See Hints.) When the employee observes someone he believes is stealing, he does not approach the suspect, but contacts security or appropriately trained staff. (Normally, a company would tell employees who to contact in theft situations.)

EXPLANATIONS

When you observe someone stealing, your first reaction might be to confront the person. That's wrong and that's dangerous. You probably aren't being paid to police the environment; certainly your job isn't to put your health on the line. No shoplifting situation is serious enough to place yourself in danger. The bottom line is that you need to let the professionals handle these situations, since they will be better trained in theft management and suspect apprehension techniques. Follow whatever procedures your company has mapped out for you, but you are far better off not intervening directly unless you are a trained security professional. (1)

HINTS

Keep in mind that, regardless of size or age, any person may carry a weapon or something that can be used as a weapon. That's a major reason why you should not approach a suspected criminal, regardless of size, age, or gender.

You may take personal offense to someone who may be stealing in your department or jurisdiction and that's understandable. You might feel obligated to take direct action and confront. Don't. Put aside your outrage or anger and let the professionals handle it.

See Also: 32. When a Customer Threatens Bodily Harm or Property Damage, 36. When a Customer Refuses to Leave

40. When a Customer Is Playing to an Audience of Other Customers

THE SITUATION

In offices open to the public, you may come across a situation where an angry or upset customer "plays to the audience" of other customers. The presence of an audience can increase the severity of the customer's angry behavior, and can also increase the length of the angry outburst. One way you can determine whether the angry person is playing to the audience is to observe whether he is glancing at the onlookers, or speaking to them. Here's a way of dealing with this situation.

TECHNIQUES USED

- Empathy Statements (1)
- Privacy and Confidentiality (2)
- Disengaging (3)

DIALOGUE

This discussion occurs in a government office, more specifically in a public waiting area that has several customer service windows. There are about 10 customers waiting and one customer is angry and interacting with the employee and playing to the audience.

Customer: You have no right to disallow my permit. Look at all these people.... I bet you're screwing over all of them. [turning to the waiting room] Isn't that right? [turns back to employee] I bet if we took a vote of all these good people, they would agree with me.

Employee: I can see that you disagree with the decision and that you are upset and want to talk about this. (1)

It's not very private here and I'm sure you don't want your personal information heard by others, so why don't I arrange to talk about this so your confidentiality is protected? If you want to step this way, we can continue the discussion. [guides customer to a room or other area away from other customers] (2)

When the customer is seated in the private area, the employee continues.

Employee: I'm going to get your file, so we can look at whether we missed something in deciding about your permit. It will just take a minute. Can I get you a cup of coffee or water?

Customer: Coffee, black, please.

Employee: [goes to get file and coffee and returns in less than two minutes] (3)

EXPLANATIONS

The employee recognizes that so long as there is an audience, the customer is going to continue to complain angrily, hoping to get moral support from the audience. First, the employee uses the front-line response, empathy statements, as a preliminary way to begin the defusing process. (1) She then takes action to remove the "audience effect," by suggesting the conversation continue in a venue that "protects the confidentiality of the customer." (2) Make special note of the way she presents this option, suggesting it ostensibly for the protection of the customer.

Once they have moved into the more private area, she uses the disengagement technique. (3) Angry people will often calm down if they have a few moments to themselves, particularly if they realize they have acted inappropriately or uncharacteristically. The employee leaves the customer alone for a few minutes, after offering two reasonable explanations for leaving the area (files and coffee), while demonstrating consideration for a "guest."

HINTS

A disengagement allows both parties (employee and customer) the opportunity to calm down and pull things together. You can use disengagement when you find you are getting overly frustrated and need time to recover.

When arranging for more privacy, keep in mind that safety is an important concern, particularly with a customer who seems unstable, is exceedingly abusive, or has a record of verbal or physical violence. For this reason, it's often best to use a location that is not completely isolated. For example, if you take the customer to an office, it may be best to keep the door open.

See Also: 41. When Customer Exhibits Passive-Aggressive Behavior, 42. When a Customer Uses Nonverbal Attempts to Intimidate

41. When a Customer Exhibits Passive-Aggressive Behavior

THE SITUATION

The passive-aggressive customer can be exceedingly frustrating to deal with, and in some cases, a passive-aggressive person can be more intimidating than someone who is overtly and obviously hostile. Luckily, most passive-aggressives are...well passive, and are unlikely to do anything that is truly dangerous.

Before we discuss what you can do with passive-aggressive customers, we need to be clear about what the term means. Passive-aggressives are uncomfortable with expressing their anger in clear and obvious ways, and choose to get their angry message across more subtly, through the use of voice tone, non-verbals like staring and glaring, rolling of eyes and sarcasm.

TECHNIQUES USED

- Not Taking the Bait (1)
- Acknowledge Customer's Needs (2)
- Assurances of Results (3)

DIALOGUE

In this situation, the customer wants to return some merchandize. There is really no problem with the return process, but this customer is exceedingly passive-aggressive, and makes his displeasure known through "passive" behavior.

Customer: [Stands in front of employee with arms crossed, glaring at employee while he makes his return request]

Employee: I bet you want to get this done quickly. (1,2) If you can just fill in the top part of this form, we'll get your refund.

Customer: Yeah. Right. More paperwork. [begins to fill out the form, and when completed waves it in front of employee and says] There, here's your form.

Employee: Good. I'll just get the manager to approve this. It will be just a minute. (1,3)

Customer: Uh huh. That will be the day.

EXPLANATIONS

In this scenario the employee knows that the customer is upset, or at least in a bad mood, and the customer insists on showing it in a rather covert way. The problem with the passive-aggressive is that if you ask about or comment upon the customer's negative feelings, the customer will deny them. So, it's best to ignore these childish, passive-aggressive behaviors. The employee simply refused to take the bait throughout the interaction. (1)

The employee also acknowledged the customer's apparent need to get the refund quickly (2), and assures the customer the refund will be processed almost on the spot.

HINTS

Passive-aggressive behavior on the part of a customer is different than passive-aggressive behavior coming from someone closer to you—let's say a spouse, child, co-worker or boss. In the latter cases, it's important, for the purposes of building and maintaining relationships, to deal with the person's discomfort. With a customer, it's usually not worth exploring why the customer is upset. The passive-aggressive customer won't tell you.

Deal with the passive-aggressive in a calm, business-like and task-oriented way. Don't take the bait, and don't indicate the behavior is putting you off balance.

Passive-aggressive behavior tends to be fairly ingrained in people who use it. You won't be able to change that in casual encounters with customers. Get the business done, and move on. The customer may still be angry or upset, but unless he or she takes some responsibility to work with you to become less upset, there's nothing you can do.

See Also: 42. When a Customer Uses Nonverbal Attempts to Intimidate

42. When a Customer Uses Nonverbal Attempts to Intimidate

THE SITUATION

When some people get angry, they will use some specific nonverbal techniques to make the other person feel uncomfortable, threatened, or cornered. These techniques include staring and glaring, invading personal space (getting too close), and using height differences to force the other person to look upwards (a subservient position). There are some ways to counter these behaviors. Here's an example.

TECHNIQUES USED

- Managing Height Differentials/Nonverbals (1)
- Distraction (2)

DIALOGUE

This situation occurs in a garage, where the customer is having his car examined to get an estimate of damage for an insurance claim after an accident. The insurance adjuster is a female, about five foot two inches tall; the man who owns the car is about six foot three. The two are standing face to face as the adjuster is outlining the damage she has identified. The customer moves closer and closer, into her personal space, which also forces the adjuster to angle her head upwards more and more.

Employee: I'm seeing some rear bumper and headlight damage on the right, but I need to get the car on a hoist to take a look at the suspension.

Customer: [glaring and moving closer] What the hell are you talking about? Any idiot can see that the suspension is shot.

Employee: [shifts a quarter turn away from the customer, breaking eye contact for a moment] (1) Mr. Smith, we'll look at the suspension in a moment, but right now, take a look at the right side panel. [points to a spot below eye level] Do you see a dent there? We don't want to miss anything. (2)

Customer: [bends down, breaking eye contact and moving out of the employee's personal space] Yes, I think I do.

EXPLANATIONS

When the customer moves into her space, the adjuster faces a dilemma. If she moves backwards, she sends a message that the customer is intimidating her and controlling the interaction. If she moves forwards, into a confrontational position, she increases the risk of more anger and even physical violence, particularly if any contact is made, however accidental. So, she turns her body to one side, so she is at a 90-degree angle to the customer (1). This position is much less confrontational than a face-to-face situation and she can also break eye contact without appearing subservient. When a person breaks eye contact at the same time as he or she moves, it appears less "weak."

At about the same time, she uses the distraction technique (2), directing the attention of the customer away from her, away from his anger, and toward a specific and concrete point. That causes the customer to look at that point (the car panel). When he bends to look, he is now lower and has lost his dominating physical position. In that stance, he can no longer stare (extend eye contact).

HINTS

When you face a person invading your space, it's never good to move closer, because of the possibility of violence. This applies whether you are bigger, smaller, or the same size.

If someone tries to intimidate by moving closer and towering over you while you are seated, then you need to get out of your chair. Do so slowly and without placing the palms of your hands on your knees or the arms of the chair, since those actions can be construed as aggressive.

The distraction technique is exceedingly valuable whenever you deal with an angry customer. You can direct his or her attention to any physical object—a computer screen, pamphlet, other piece of paper, clipboard, etc. However, you *must* direct his or her attention verbally—"Take a look at this because ... "—and nonverbally—point to the specific spot you want the customer to look at. The distraction technique will not work if you simply provide something and say, "Please look at this."

See Also: 41. When Customer Exhibits Passive-Aggressive Behavior, 43. When a Customer Makes Persistent and Frequent Phone Calls

43. When a Customer Makes Persistent and Frequent Phone Calls

THE SITUATION

A customer who calls over and over again when there is no clear constructive point in doing so is enough to drive any employee to frustration. Customers do this kind of thing for various reasons—perhaps in the hope of being so annoying the employee will give them the answer they want or simply because they are exceedingly anxious. Apart from being annoying, the bigger problem is that persistent and pointless phone calls interfere with getting real work done and serving other customers. While you can't really control who calls and how often, there are some things you can try.

TECHNIQUES USED

- Broken Record (1)
- Acknowledge Customer's Needs (2)
- Finding Agreement Points (3)
- Setting Limits (4)

DIALOGUE

In this situation, the caller wants to speak to the manager, who is away from his desk for most of the day. During the first call, the employee who answers explains that the manager will be unable to return the call today, but will likely do so tomorrow. Unfortunately, about 30 minutes later the customer calls again, asking if the manager is in yet.

Customer: This is John Smith. I called earlier, but I need to know if the manager is back yet.

Employee: As I said, he won't be available until at least tomorrow. I will make sure he knows you urgently want to talk to him. (1)

Customer: OK. Bye.

About an hour later, the customer calls again and repeats the question.

Employee: Mr. Smith, I realize you are anxious to speak to the manager and I've promised you I'll convey a sense of urgency to him. (1, 2) You can save yourself a lot of time by waiting until you hear from us tomorrow, and I'd really like to ask you to refrain from calling until tomorrow.

Customer: Yeah, well, I'll do what I want.

Employee: I'm sure you will. (3) If you do call back today, though, your call is simply going to get routed to voice mail. Best to wait until tomorrow. (4)

EXPLANATIONS

This is a difficult situation because the customer controls whether he calls back or not; the employee can only encourage restraint. The basic approach is to avoid getting into an argument by doing a "broken record" of the same message—that the manager is not available and will call tomorrow. (1)

Despite this, the customer calls back again, asking the same question. Once again the employee uses the broken record (1), but couples this with an acknowledgment that the caller feels the situation is urgent. (2) The customer does not respond favorably and indicates he will do what he wants. Rather than arguing, the employee agrees that he can do as he pleases. (3)

The employee also sets a limit. (4) He indicates that further calls will not be answered and will simply go to voice mail. In other words, he is trying to get across the point that additional calls will simply waste the caller's time. Of course, if the employee lacks the facility to do this (caller ID), then this particular consequence won't work.

A second option for setting limits goes like this. "I appreciate that you want to speak to the manager, but if you call again today, I'm not going to be able to speak to you, except to repeat what I've already told you." And then enforce that consequence/limit.

HINTS

The worst thing you can do is get angry or let your frustration show, since this will almost always precipitate an argument, which will eat up more of your time.

You can explain why you can't continue to respond to the same questions, but the challenge is to do so in a way that does not send the message that you have "more important things to do." If the customer gets that message from you, whether implicit or explicit, an argument is likely.

See Also: 14. When a Customer Won't Stop Talking on the Phone, 23. When You Need to Route a Customer Phone Call

44. When Someone Else Is Not Responding (No Callback)

THE SITUATION

In the workplace, we all work with and depend upon other employees. Unfortunately, colleagues may not return calls in a prompt manner, or fulfill their commitments to customers. On occasion you may run into a situation where you receive a call from a customer complaining that one of your colleagues has not responded to phone messages from the customer. Since the customer has managed to contact you, it's likely he's going to vent his frustration on you. How do you deal with this situation, particularly without casting aspersions on your colleague?

TECHNIQUES USED

- Empathy Statements (1)
- You're Right! (2)
- Providing Explanations (3)
- Offering Choices/Empowerment (4)
- Arranging Follow-Up (5)
- Apologize (6)

DIALOGUE

In this situation, the caller has been trying to get in touch with Bob, and has left several urgent messages requesting that Bob return his call. He manages to call you.

Customer: I've left at least three messages for Bob, in the last two days, and I haven't heard from him. What kind of outfit are you running here? Doesn't anyone return calls?

Employee: That's got to be frustrating for you. (1) We try to ensure that all calls are returned within one working day, but obviously something has gone awry. Let me check to see whether Bob has been in, or perhaps he's been sick. (3)

Customer: Even if he's sick, shouldn't someone be covering his calls? Or don't you follow proper business practice.

Employee: You're right! (2) Whatever the circumstances, you should have received a return phone call. I'm checking right now to see if Bob is in. Yes, he just returned from a meeting. I'll tell you what. (3) If you give me your name, and what you are calling about, I'll walk down the hall, and explain the situation to Bob. If Bob can't call you within an hour, I'll see if someone else can. One way or another, someone will call you within the hour, let's say by 5:30. Is that Ok? (4)

Customer: No, it's not OK. I want to know what's happening now, before I hang up.

Employee: I can do that. If I can place you on hold, I'll talk to Bob right away, or I can call you back in five minutes. (4)

Customer: Ok. Call me back then.

The employee ends the conversation by apologizing, then speaks to Bob. Whatever the outcome, the employee personally calls Bob back (5,6) (following up), and tries to solve the customer's problem.

EXPLANATIONS

These situations can be frustrating because both you and the customer may be quite annoyed because of someone else's behavior over which neither of you have control. As with most irate customer situations, the employee begins the response with an empathy statement (1), and then explains that the company strives to call customers back within one business day. (3) Notice the explanation about callbacks is kept short, because the truth is that the company policy is of little relevance to the customer at this point in time.

When the customer points out that someone ought to be covering the phone for an absent employee or one taken ill, the employee takes the opportunity to use the "You're Right!" technique. (2)

The next part of the conversation is directed at trying to solve the customer's immediate problem—getting in touch with Bob, or someone else who can help him as soon as possible. The employee offers alternatives so the customer gets to choose what would be best for him from a range of possible options. (4)

Finally, the conversation ends after an agreement has been struck about follow-up (5), and with the employee offering an apology. Needless to say the employee (or someone) *must* follow up in the agreed upon fashion, or risk the customer going from irate and frustrated to full bore angry.

HINTS

It is very important that you do not make any disparaging remarks about the coworker who has not returned the call, even if that coworker has a history of this kind of behavior. For example: "Oh, Bob is always late returning calls" is completely inappropriate and puts Bob, your company, *and* you in a negative light. It can also cause problems with your coworker.

The more you can go above and beyond the call of duty in resolving this difficulty, the better. You can't necessarily deflect the customer's anger resulting from a sloppy colleague, but you can act in ways so that you won't get painted with the same brush.

See Also: 56. When a Reservation/Appointment Is Lost and You Cannot Meet the Commitment, 58. When a Customer Complains About a Known Problem

45. When You Need to Clarify Commitments

THE SITUATION

Customer service isn't always a one-way street where the employee is the only one with commitments to keep. There are situations where both you and the customer have to do certain things to meet the customer's needs. While this situation exists in normal interactions with customers, it's far more frequent when you are working with internal clients.

TECHNIQUES USED

■ Summarize the Conversation (1)
■ Probing Questions (2)

DIALOGUE

Over the course of this conversation, the employee has committed to developing a formal proposal to be forwarded to the client. Since the proposal is based on information that must first be sent from the client to the employee, the client also has to make and keep a commitment to get the material sent to the employee. The conversation below is an example of clarifying and summarizing commitments.

Customer: So, you're going to get the proposal to me by the end of the week, right?

Employee: Yes, but I can do that only if you send me the portfolio information by fax sometime today. Can you do that?

Customer: Yes, I'll do that.

Employee: OK, let's make sure we are on absolutely the same wavelength. You're going to send me the portfolio by fax. That document includes [details]. I should receive that today. Then I'll use that to draft a proposal that includes [details] and get it to you by the end of the week. Is that what we are saying? (1)

Customer: Yes.

Employee: Good. One more thing. I don't see anything that might cause me to be unable to get the proposal done on time. Is there anything that might come up that might interfere with your getting the portfolio here? (2)

EXPLANATIONS

This is a relatively straightforward discussion that includes a bit of negotiating and the use of a basic communication technique to avoid the consequences of misunderstanding. The initial part of the conversation involves both parties agreeing to meet some specific commitments by specific deadlines. In this scenario, both parties must keep their commitments in order for the customer to receive the proposal he wants. Once the initial agreement is made, the employee summarizes the conversation. (1) This might seem like overkill to you, but it's always better to err on the cautious side. Making sure communication is working is better than running the risk of a project going askew due to a misunderstanding.

At the end of the conversation, you'll notice the employee doing something interesting. He uses a probing question (2), asking whether the customer can foresee any possible barriers to keeping his commitment to fax the material. Why? Because sometimes people will make commitments to do something without actually thinking enough about the commitment. By using this probing question, the employee encourages the customer to think a little more carefully. Since the employee's ability to keep his end of the bargain is dependent on the customer keeping his commitments, it makes sense to do that.

HINTS

Whenever commitments are made, the conversation should end with a summary of those commitments.

See Also: 12. When the Customer Needs to Follow a Sequence of Actions, 51. When an Internal Customer Isn't Following Procedures to Request Service

THE SITUATION

Customers will sometimes ask for information that you are not permitted to give out, because it might compromise the privacy of others, pose a security threat, or result in the sharing of proprietary information the company does not allow to be circulated. The trick here is to refuse in a professional and polite way that is less likely to create a long, drawn-out argument.

TECHNIQUES USED

- Acknowledge Customer's Needs (1)
- Explain Reasoning or Actions (2)
- Providing Alternatives (3)

DIALOGUE

In this short interaction, the customer asks for the home phone number of the manager of the department.

Customer: Since he's not in, I'd like to contact him at home. What's his number?

Employee: I understand you want to resolve this quickly, (1) but I'm not allowed to give out that information. Everyone deserves some time off from work and our staff isn't available for home phone calls. (2) What I can do is arrange for you to talk to someone else who is available right now who can help solve your problem. (3)

EXPLANATIONS

In this example, the employee handles the situation by acknowledging the customer's desire to deal with his problem quickly (1) and then provides a brief explanation of why she can't give out the number. (2) The reason it's good to provide an explanation is that it makes the response sound less bureaucratic or arbitrary. Finally, the employee offers an alternative (3). This tends to soften the refusal.

HINTS

When refusing, offer an explanation of why you are refusing. That sends the message that you aren't being arbitrary, but are interested in helping the customer understand the reasoning behind the refusal.

Explanations should be short, followed by offering some sort of alternative that might address the customer's needs.

See Also: 20. When You Don't Have the Answer. 59. When a Customer Asks Inappropriate Questions

47. When a Customer Makes a Suggestion to Improve Service

THE SITUATION

One of the best ways to find out how to improve customer service is to get information from customers. In this situation, a customer volunteers a suggestion about how to improve the service at a bank.

TECHNIQUES USED

- Thank-Yous (1)
- Arranging Follow-Up (2)
- Closing Interactions Positively (3)

DIALOGUE

Sometimes employees will encounter customers who make suggestions for how to improve service. Because employees are often not trained to do anything with these suggestions, they will listen politely hoping the person will finish what he or she has to say so they can get on with finishing a transaction. It doesn't have to be that way as this dialogue shows. Listening to such suggestions and then in fact acting on them can affect both your relationship with customers and improve your ability to serve them.

Customer: You know, when I come to this branch at lunch, I'm always surprised that you have less staff during the period most people come to the bank. I'd bet you'd do much better by making sure there are more tellers on at lunchtime.

Employee: Thanks for the suggestion. I happen to agree and I know this issue has come up before. What I'd like to do is pass your suggestion on to the manager of the branch, since she's the one that would have to arrange more staff. And, if you like, I can also have the manager follow up with you on your suggestion, if only to explain why it might not be practical. Is that something you'd like?

Customer: Well, yes, I'd appreciate that. My name and phone number are ….

Employee: OK. It might be a few days before you hear from Marsha Smith, who is our manager. I also appreciate that you thought enough about us to offer a suggestion about how we can provide better service to you. Have a good day. (3)

EXPLANATIONS

This is a relatively straightforward situation, because the customer is making a suggestion in a constructive and neutral way. The employee thanks the customer for the suggestion (1). What's more critical here is the employee's offer and commitment to pass the suggestion on to the branch manager and arrange for follow-up if the customer desires it (2). Why is this so important? Because it tells the customer that the employee is taking her seriously and that she is important to the employee and the branch.

Finally, at the end of the interaction, you see an effective "close," where the employee reiterates an appreciation of the customer's time and effort in offering up the suggestion.

HINTS

When you make a commitment on behalf of someone else (in this case the bank manager), be absolutely sure that the other person will keep the commitment you made.

When you make a commitment for someone else, it's always a good idea for *you* to follow up with the person who is supposed to fulfill the commitment. In this case the employee would talk with or remind the bank manager to contact the customer in a day or two.

It's good customer service to treat *every* suggestion as important, even those that seem impractical or "poor." Above all, don't argue.

See Also: 49. When You Are Following Up on a Customer Complaint, 53. When You Want Feedback from the Customer

48. When You Can't Find a Customer's Reservation/Appointment

THE SITUATION

In any business where the customer needs to make a reservation or appointment to be served, there's always a risk or possibility that the reservation or appointment information may be lost. How you recover from this situation means the difference between a satisfied customer and one who might complain, argue, vent, and otherwise take up a lot of your time.

Situations like this can occur with airlines, hotels, restaurants, doctors' or dentists' offices, or similar environments.

TECHNIQUES USED

- Apologize (1)
- Assurances of Results (2)
- Bonus Buyoff (3)
- You're Right! (4)
- Contact Security/Authorities/Management (5)

DIALOGUE

This situation takes place in a hotel lobby. The customer arrives with a reservation number, but the hotel clerk has no record of the reservation. In this example, the employee can accommodate the customer's needs, but perhaps not without some degree of inconvenience for the customer.

Customer: What the heck do you mean, you can't find my reservation? I made it at least two weeks ago.

Employee: I'm sorry for the inconvenience, (1) but it shouldn't be a problem to get you into a room even without the reservation. (2) It should only take a minute or two…. I just need to get some information from you and, once we're done, I'll find out what we can do to compensate you for the inconvenience. (3)

Customer: Well, this is stupid. It just shouldn't happen.

Employee: You're right, (4) it shouldn't, and once we get you settled I'll let my manager know about the problem so we can do our best to make sure it doesn't happen again. (5)

EXPLANATIONS

Since the company has probably made an error, the first step is to apologize (1). It's possible the customer has made the error, but even in the case where the customer has arrived at the wrong time or place, it's best to assume the company has made the mistake, since arguing will alienate the customer and waste more time.

In this situation, there is a vacancy, so the problem is relatively minor. The employee wants to communicate as quickly as possible that the customer *will* be accommodated and the inconvenience will be minor (2).

The employee suggests that the hotel will offer some sort of compensation, or bonus buyoff (3), as a concrete indication that the hotel is truly sorry for any inconvenience. The employee may need to follow through on this, perhaps talking with the manager on duty to determine the exact nature of the compensation.

The employee uses the "You're right" technique (4), emphasizing that she agrees with the customer that this should never have happened. By following this up with a promise to contact/notify management that the reservation was lost (5), she solidifies the customer's perception that the employee and the hotel take these problems seriously. Because the employee does this, it's more likely the customer will return to the hotel.

HINTS

Customers sometimes get confused about their reservations or blame their own error on the company. While it may seem unfair to take responsibility for a problem that is not your fault, that was really caused by the customer, nothing is gained by arguing with the customer or focusing on who is to blame.

Even if you are not personally responsible for a mistake, apologize on behalf of the company.

See Also: 56. When a Reservation/Appointment Is Lost and You Cannot Meet the Commitment, 58. When a Customer Complains About a Known Problem

49. When You Are Following Up on a Customer Complaint

THE SITUATION

Believe it or not, one of the biggest opportunities to show a customer how much you value him or her involves how you recover when the customer has a complaint. Of course, if you can address the customer's complaint immediately, that is a major and critical step. What most companies and people don't realize is that following up on customer complaints can complete the recovery cycle, and transform a complaining customer into a customer for life.

TECHNIQUES USED

- Use Customer's Name (1)
- Offering Choices/Empowering (2)
- Probing Questions (3)
- Thank Yous (4)
- Above and Beyond the Call of Duty (5)

DIALOGUE

In this case, the manager of a retail outlet has employees notify him of any significant complaints on the part of customers, along with any contact information the customer is willing to offer. Here's how the manager follows up on complaints via phone calls.

Manager: Mr. Jones (1), this is John Roberts from the Loveme Emporium. You may remember about a month ago you had some concerns about [describe situation] , and I'm phoning to see how everything worked out, and if you are satisfied with the result. Have you got a minute? (2)

Customer: Sure. What did you want to know?

Manager: Well, let's start with whether you were satisfied with the outcome? (3)

Customer: Yes and no. I'm satisfied that we got things solved, but I have to tell you that the whole process took far too much time—time I didn't have to waste.

Manager: I can understand what you are saying. Is there anything specific we could have done to shorten the time? (3)

Customer: [offers some suggestions]

Manager: Thank you for the ideas. (4) I'm going to pass those on to the District Manager. Here's something I can suggest to you right now though. If you ever come across a similar situation, please feel free to contact me directly at 555-1212 or in person. I hope this doesn't happen again, but if it does, I can make sure it's settled much more quickly in the future. (5)

Customer: Well, thank you. You know, it's pretty rare to get this kind of personal contact from anyone these days. I'm impressed.

EXPLANATIONS

The techniques used here are fairly straightforward. First, we have the basic courtesy ones; using the customer's name (1), and Thank Yous (4). In addition, you can see that the manager asks permission (choices/empowerment) to give the customer the option of answering a few questions or not. (2)

However, the critical component here is (5) where the manager goes above and beyond the call of duty by offering the customer "special" access in the event that a similar problem occurs. It reassures the customer that the phone call is sincere, and that the manager is offering something significant to help him.

What really makes this kind of follow-up succeed is that the customer perceives that he is getting very personalized service. To this end, the manager used his name, and demonstrated that he took the time to familiarize himself with, and remember the customer and his situation. Personalized service is so rare these days that customers who receive it can become very loyal indeed.

HINTS

When following up on a complaint, it's absolutely essential that the person following up take the time to familiarize himself with the customer's situation, *and* prove to the customer that he has put in the time to do so. That's where the power of the follow-up lies.

While this example focuses on a manager following up, non-management employees should be encouraged to do this. It's a low cost way of demonstrating to customers that they are important.

See Also: 47. When a Customer Makes a Suggestion to Improve Service, 55. When You Need to Respond to a Customer Complaint Made in Writing

50. Properly Identifying the Internal Customer

THE SITUATION

When working with internal customers it's important that you identify who has the power and authority to make decisions, and that you interact directly with that person. Sometimes you may be approached by someone who lacks the decision-making power that will permit you to help the customer. Here's a process you can use to identify the real customer, and request direct contact.

TECHNIQUES USED

- Probing Questions (1)
- Active Listening (2)
- Questioning Instead of Stating (3)
- Explain Reasoning or Actions (4)

DIALOGUE

In this situation the employee works in the Information Technology Division (IT). He is approached by someone from the Insurance Division about a software development project the Insurance Division needs. The IT employee is not clear about who the real customer/decision-maker will be and seeks to identify and contact that person.

Employee: Fred, I know that projects of this size usually have a lot of people who need to be involved and considered. Before we move forward we need to involve those other people. (4) Can you suggest who needs to be involved in our discussions? (1)

Customer: Sure, I'm the lead person on this. Then, there's the Supervisor of Underwriting. Also, my manager needs to sign off on the project.

Employee: OK, so what you are saying is that, ultimately, your manager is the one who is the final decision-maker. Is that right? (2)

Customer: Yes, ultimately, but I make the recommendations to my manager, so pretty much what I suggest is accepted.

Employee: OK. That makes sense. I want to make sure that we get this project on the right path and don't have to redo things, so I'd like to arrange a meeting with your manager. (4) Can we do that? (3)

EXPLANATIONS

This example is a bit trickier than it looks. The employee wants to be careful not to alienate the customer she is interacting with, by insinuating that he is incompetent or the wrong person. That's why she uses a gentle approach, rather than a more direct approach.

The employee uses some gentle probing questions (1) to get the customer to identify the key players. Even though the employee knows the answer, it's a good tactic to encourage the customer to identify the other players that if only to confirm the employee's understanding is accurate. To put the question in context, the employee explains the reasoning behind the question (4).

After the customer provides information regarding other people that need to be involved, the employee uses an active listening response (2) to show she is paying attention and to confirm that she understands the customer's response.

Once again, the employee explains why the manager

should be involved (4) and follows up by asking a question, "Can we do that?", rather than making a direct request or demand. The employee does this to avoid the possibility the customer will feel demeaned or marginalized.

HINTS

People don't always feel comfortable admitting they don't have the power or authority to complete an arrangement. You need to be aware of that and use gentle probing questions to identify who really has the authority.

Since you may work with the same internal customers over long periods of time, remember that you have two concerns. One is to get the project going and meet the needs of the customer. The other, which is as important, is to build relationships with those internal customers and avoid poisoning those relationships by being too aggressive or task-oriented.

See Also: 45. When You Need to Clarify Commitments, 51. When an Internal Customer Isn't Following Procedures to Request Service

51. When an Internal Customer Isn't Following Procedures to Request Service

THE SITUATION

Internal customers, due to their familiarity with staff, sometimes go directly to an employee to ask for help, when they should be making a formal request for service. This can complicate life for the unit providing the service, since it makes it difficult to coordinate requests. What do you do if you are approached directly to provide service, but your work unit requires that the internal customer make a formal request?

TECHNIQUES USED

- Providing Explanations (1)
- Empathy Statements (2)
- Expediting (3)

DIALOGUE

In this situation, a member of the Accounting Department (internal customer) contacts a computer technician in the Information Technology (IT) Department. IT has a set of procedures it wants internal clients to use so it can coordinate and prioritize requests.

Customer: Our computers have been down for about 20 minutes and we can't process our month-end invoices. It's a real mess. Can you come up and see what the problem is?

Employee: That's a pretty serious problem. (2) We need to get on this right away, but I'll need you to complete a request for service form and get it to our job coordinator.

Customer: We don't have time for that stuff. I need this fixed yesterday. Can't you just come up and take a look?

Employee: I'll tell you what. We can get something moving on this within the hour if you get the request for service done. How about if I come up right now and get the request for service form, and I'll hand-walk it to the coordinator for approval? (3) The whole thing should take about 10 minutes.

Customer: Well, I don't see why that's necessary, since we're talking right now and you're the one that has to fix the problem.

Employee: I understand it's frustrating. (2) Let me explain why we want to have a formal request. [explains] (1)

Customer: OK. I guess that makes sense. Can you come up right now?

EXPLANATIONS

It's easy to understand why the Accounting Department employee is upset and concerned, because it appears that he is being tied up in red tape. It's also easy to understand why the IT department needs to coordinate and prioritize service. In this situation, the IT employee knows that this *will* be a high-priority job, provided the formal request is made.

Notice the use of empathy statements (2) by the employee to show concern and understanding. What's really important in this example is the promise of immediate help (expediting) (3). By offering to get things going immediately, the employee is sending the message that the customer's needs will be met and the employee will help the customer navigate the process of making a formal request. Finally, you can see that the customer isn't understanding why the request is necessary. The employee explains the reasons for the procedure (1).

HINTS

When explaining the purpose of a policy or procedure, it's important to highlight any benefits of the procedure from the point of view of the customer or customers.

Explain policies or procedures in plain language without using jargon. The exception is when the customer is conversant with the jargon.

See Also: 12. When a Customer Needs to Follow a Sequence of Actions, 50. Properly Identifying the Internal Customer

52. When the Customer Wants Something That Won't Fill His Need

THE SITUATION

You may find yourself in a situation where the customer thinks he wants something that you know will not make him happy or fill an important need he has expressed. While you might think that giving the customer what he wants is generally a good thing, it may not be so in this situation. Your role should be to make sure the customer remains happy over time. Here's how to help the customer make a better choice.

TECHNIQUES USED

- Active Listening (1)
- Probing Questions (2)

DIALOGUE

In this situation, which takes place in an automobile dealership, the customer has expressed a strong concern about the importance of fuel efficiency, but has also indicated he wants a sports utility vehicle (which has particularly poor fuel efficiency). The employee uses questions to help the customer clarify his priorities.

Employee: OK. If I understand what you are saying, you would like a fuel-efficient SUV, maybe a Blazer. Is that correct? (1)

Customer: Yes. I really like the Blazer.

Employee: I want to be sure you won't be disappointed in whatever choice you make, so let me ask you a few questions. First, given the mileage you've said you drive, the Blazer will cost you about $250 per month in fuel.

On the other hand, going to a smaller hatchback like the Sentra would cost you about $80 a month in fuel. Are you comfortable paying that extra money every month for the Blazer? (2)

Customer: Wow. It's that much difference?

Employee: Yes. So which is most important to you, having something that's more fuel-efficient or having the extra space of the Blazer? (2)

Customer: Well, I like the Blazer, but I'm not sure I really need one. On the other hand, I don't want to be spending over $3,000 in gas each year. Maybe we should look at those other vehicles. You're suggesting that a Sentra might be a good way to go, right?

EXPLANATIONS

Notice that the first step in this example involves the use of active listening, reflecting back what the customer has said to ensure that the employee understands (1). An additional benefit of this is that the customer knows the employee is paying attention.

The probing questions used here are an alternative to the employee offering expert advice and pros and cons directly. While the latter techniques can be useful or combined with the use of probing questions, the advantage of the probing questions lies in gently leading the customer to consider issues he may not be thinking about. The employee is helping the customer to "connect the dots."

HINTS

Probing questions can be used in conjunction with expert recommendations and a more direct discussion of pros and cons. When combined, usually the probing questions would be used first.

Active listening is almost always a good technique to use in all kinds of situations. What's important is that the active listening responses sound natural and comfortable. Active listening responses should never sound artificial, or too "touchy-feely."

See Also: 33. When a Customer is Confused About What He or She Wants or Needs

53. When You Want Feedback from the Customer

THE SITUATION

We usually think of customer service as the process of providing something—services, information or products *to* the customer. There's another component of customer service, and that involves the process of getting feedback *from* the customer so you can improve how you provide for the customer. Most people involved in serving customers don't think of this as part of their jobs, but it can be useful. How do you elicit feedback that might help you and your company improve service?

TECHNIQUES USED

- Offering Choices/Empowering (1)
- Probing Questions (2)
- Active Listening (3)
- Arranging Follow-Up (4)
- Use Customer's Name (5)
- Thank Yous (6)

DIALOGUE

The setting is a bank. The employee wants to find out (with the support of the manager), how customers see the service they are receiving, and whether they have any suggestions or comments for improvement. Here's how she does it.

Employee: Mrs. Jones (5), we're interested in hearing what you think about our service at this branch. If you have just a minute or two, I'd appreciate it if you could answer some quick questions. Is that OK? (1)

Customer: Sure. If it's short.

Employee: Yes, it's short. On a scale of one to ten how would you rate the service you receive at this branch? (2)

Customer: Well, I guess a six.

Employee: Is there anything specific that we could do to raise that rating?

Customer: Well, yes. The thing that gets me is that I always come in at lunch time, and it seems that's when you have the most people waiting, and the least number of tellers working.

Employee: So, if we could reduce the waiting at lunch time, that would help? (3)

Customer: Yes, it would.

Employee: [asks one or two other short questions] Well, thank you Mrs. Jones (5). I'm passing these suggestions on to our bank manager, and if you like, I can follow up with you to let you know the result. Would you like that? (4,1)

Customer: Well, no, that's not necessary. I'm in every week, so I can talk to you then.

Employee: OK, well thanks again.

EXPLANATIONS

This is a fairly straight-forward process. Make special note that the employee offers the customer the choice of answering the questions or not (1), and uses the same technique at the end of the interaction to determine if the customer wants to be contacted. It's about offering choices.

When asking for information from customers, it's best to provide some form of follow-up option. (4) This tells the customer that you (and your organization) are sincere about the information the customer provides, and that you are willing to try to do something to accommodate the needs of the customer. It moves the feedback process beyond "just talking."

You can also see the use of two techniques that should be part of almost all customer interactions—common courtesy. They are using the customer's name (5), and using thank yous. (6)

HINTS

The same basic techniques can be used if your company has some form of feedback form customers can fill out, and drop off.

Collecting feedback from customers, and then doing nothing—no feedback and no fixing of problems, is worse than collecting no feedback at all. That's because it will seem phony to customers. If you collect feedback on your own initiative, make sure you pass the information on to those in your organization that should have the information.

See Also: 47. When a Customer Makes a Suggestion to Improve Service, 55. When You Need to Respond to a Customer Complaint Made in Writing

54. When a Customer Complains About Red Tape and Paperwork

THE SITUATION

All organizations have policies, procedures, and paperwork. Some organizations, particularly those associated with government, seem to have inordinate amounts of red tape involved in getting things done. Customers often get frustrated at the paperwork and red tape needed to accomplish something and may vent their frustration on you. How do you deal with this situation?

TECHNIQUES USED

- Active Listening (1)
- Providing Explanations (2)
- Empathy Statements (3)
- Some People Think That (Neutral Mode) (4)
- Offering Choices/Empowering (5)
- Broken Record (6)

DIALOGUE

This situation occurs in a government office, but could occur in any organization that has fairly complex procedures and requires filling out lots of forms (e.g., banks and medical facilities). Here, the customer wants to apply for a driver's license. We join the conversation in progress.

Employee: OK. Let me explain the process. I need a copy of your birth certificate and one other piece of ID, and then we need to schedule your written test and your driving test.

Customer: What? This is going to take forever. I went through all that three years ago. Why the hell do I have to do it all over again?

Employee: I understand that you don't want to go through that again, (1) but the problem is that you haven't had a valid license in two years, so it's like starting over again. (2)

Customer: What a pile of crap! You government folks will do anything to make things hard for us taxpayers. I pay your salary, you know.

Employee: I know it's frustrating. (3) Some people do think that the laws are strict, (4) but you know, they are there to protect everyone and to make sure the streets are as safe as we can make them. (2)

Customer: Well, it's just plain stupid.

Employee: It's up to you what you want to do. If you would like to speak to my supervisor, I can arrange that, or we can go ahead and set up the appointments. Which would you prefer? (5)

Customer: Neither. I don't like either.

Employee: Well, those are pretty much the options. Which would you prefer? (6)

EXPLANATIONS

The first technique used is active listening (1), where the employee tries to put herself on the same side as the customer by showing she is paying attention and understands where the customer is coming from. She follows this up by offering an explanation for the requirements (2).

When the customer expresses his frustration, the employee uses an empathy technique (3) and "neutral mode" (4) to try to soften the news.

The customer continues to make angry comments, so

the employee shifts gears to get things moving by offering two alternatives—speaking to the supervisor or making the appointments, leaving the choice to the customer (5). She does this because no amount of arguing or discussion is going to result in changes to the policies and laws, over which neither of them has control. When the customer indicates his displeasure with the options, she uses the broken record technique (6), presenting the options to him once again. She does this to push the customer into making a decision and not wasting more time arguing.

HINTS

When explaining a policy or set of procedures, it's important to do so in plain language without quoting specific laws or policy numbers. Unless asked for detailed explanations, it's best to keep explanations short and to the point.

There are situations where the red tape cannot be explained rationally. You may not know why it's necessary or it may be one of those things that really is unnecessarily complex. In that situation, it's best to admit you don't know why and offer access to someone who might be better able to explain it. In these situations, focus on placing yourself on the same side as the customer, emphasizing empathy statements and active listening.

Avoid arguing with the customer about procedural necessities. No amount of talking is going to change them, since they are beyond your control. If the customer insists on arguing, it's better to direct him or her to someone who has the authority to change the procedures.

See Also: 6. When a Customer Has a Negative Attitude About Your Company Due to Past Experiences, 7. When You Need to Explain a Company Policy or Procedure

55. When You Need to Respond to a Customer Complaint Made in Writing

THE SITUATION

A customer who complains in writing is a customer who is angry enough to take the time to write a letter. That means the person is pretty angry. The usual response is to reply in writing, but that's only part of the process of offering superior customer service.

TECHNIQUES USED

- Use Customer's Name (1)
- Explain Reasoning or Actions (2)
- Offering Choices/Empowerment (3)
- Probing Questions (4)

DIALOGUE

The employee has been asked by his manager to draft a written response to a customer complaint letter. He drafts the response, but realizes that a written response, while necessary, is not going to be sufficient to convince the customer that she is receiving top-notch service. Here are two options.

In option 1, the employee drafts a response and follows up via phone before sending the letter.

Employee: Mr. Smith, (1) this is John Jones from Acme. I'm following up on a letter you wrote outlining a concern you had about [explains what the customer wrote about]. I'm sending out a written response you should have within two days, but I wanted to talk to you personally, to clarify the situation. (2) Can I ask you a few questions? Then I can go over what's in the letter. (3)

In option 2, the employee composes the reply, sends it, and then follows up with the customer after the customer has received the reply. It goes like this.

Employee: Mr. Smith, (1) this is John Jones from Acme. I wanted to follow up on our response to your letter, to see if you had any questions about our position and where things are right now. (2) First, have you received our response? (4)

Customer: Yes, I got it today. Thanks for taking the time to call.

Employee: Was there anything in our letter that we didn't make clear? (4)

EXPLANATIONS

In both examples, the employee uses the customer's name (1) and also identifies himself. He does this to personalize the call and to show that he has made the effort to remember the name.

Also, in both examples, the employee quickly explains the purpose of the call (2). Once that's done, he basically asks permission to continue, giving the customer the choice (3). This comes across as considerate and respectful, while trying to maintain control over the interaction.

In the second example, you can see the use of probing questions (4). Again this shows that the employee and, by extension, the company, are interested in the customer's problem. The questions, particularly when he asks, "First, have you received our letter?" provide information the employee needs to guide how he handles the phone call. Clearly, if the customer has not received the letter, he needs to handle the call differently.

What's important here is that the employee, through actions and words, demonstrates that the complaint is being taken seriously and that the company wants to do all it can to address the customer's concerns.

HINTS

Responses to written complaints should be accompanied by some form of more personal follow-up. At the best of times, written words tend to come across as cold and distant.

When writing a response to a complaint, it's important to draft something that is informal and uses plain language. A common mistake is to sound stiff or bureaucratic in written responses, which guarantees the customer will be even angrier.

See Also: 7. When You Need to Explain a Company Policy or Procedure, 47. When a Customer Makes a Suggestion to Improve Service

56. When a Reservation/Appointment Is Lost and You Cannot Meet the Commitment

THE SITUATION

In dialogue 48, we dealt with a situation where the customer's reservation was lost, but the employee could accommodate the customer with only minimal inconvenience for the customer. What happens when the customer cannot be accommodated and it appears the fault lies with the company?

TECHNIQUES USED

- Preemptive Strike (1)
- Assurances of Results (2)
- Providing Alternatives (3)
- Empathy Statements (4)
- Bonus Buyoff (5)
- Contact Security/Authorities/Management (6)

DIALOGUE

As with the previous example, this occurs in a hotel. The employee discovers there is no record of the reservation and, unfortunately, the hotel is booked solid and cannot offer the customer the room that was promised.

Employee: Mr. Jones, I can't find any record of your reservation, but I can promise you that we will find a place for you to stay. (1, 2) Unfortunately, we're completely booked, but I will find you alternate accommodations that won't cost you any more than you'd spend here. (3) It may take a few minutes, but I *will* find something for you. (3)

Customer: What kind of outfit do you run here? I shouldn't have to run all over the city when I made a reservation for here.

Employee: I'd be upset too if it was me. (4) Am I correct that you want to stay in this general area? If that's the case, I'll phone around to other hotels and arrange a room close by. I can probably arrange a significant discount. (5)

Customer: Well, I guess that's better than nothing, but this should never happen.

Employee: I'm going to inform the manager about this so the next time you come to our hotel, it won't happen again. (6) Sound fair?

EXPLANATIONS

One of the key elements in this example involves assuring the customer that he will not end up with no place to stay the night. The employee addresses this issue as early as possible in the conversation, using a preemptive strike (1) and assurances of results (2). In this case, the preemptive strike involves addressing the customer's concern about having a place to stay *before* the customer expresses that concern.

The employee suggests an alternative to solve the problem (3), to "make it right." In this situation, all the words in the world aren't going to bring the customer back if the situation isn't "made right."

You might notice that while the employee is doing his best, the customer is still irate. That's typical and understandable. That's why the employee uses an empathy statement (4).

Before making calls to other local hotels to arrange for

a room, the employee "sweetens" the situation by mentioning the possibility of a bonus buyoff (5) and reassures the customer that the hotel will investigate and take every effort to prevent a recurrence. The employee promises to bring this situation to the attention of the manager (6).

HINTS

There are two prongs to this approach. One is to do everything possible to "make it right," which means finding a room and arranging things for the customer. The other is to show that the employee and the hotel take these situations seriously and that the customer and his needs are important. *Both* prongs are essential: solve the problem and, at the same time, send the "you are important" message.

While we've used a hotel example, the procedures are the same whenever the company might be at fault for a lost reservation or appointment. Minimize inconvenience. Express concern. Compensate for inconvenience. Solve the immediate problem.

See Also: 48. When You Can't Find a Customer's Reservation/Appointment, 58. When a Customer Complains About a Known Problem

57. When Customers Are Waiting in a Waiting Room

THE SITUATION

This is a situation you will relate to from the customers' perspective. It's not uncommon in this era of under-staffing and unexpected delays for customers to have to wait in a waiting room, even if they have appointments that are long past. What do you do when there are delays and you have a room full of people who have been waiting for some time?

TECHNIQUES USED

- Empathy Statements (1)
- Explain Reasoning or Actions (2)
- Apologize (3)
- Providing Alternatives (4)

DIALOGUE

This situation takes place in a doctor's office. There are about 10 people waiting to be called for their appointment. Unfortunately, the doctor is running between 30 and 50 minutes behind schedule, so some people have been waiting quite some time. Here's what the receptionist does.

Employee: [Loud voice to waiting customers] If I can have your attention for a moment, I'll explain the delay and what you can do.

Customers: [Look up]

Employee: The doctor had an emergency earlier today that caused a delay of about 45 minutes, so everyone has been pushed back. (2) I know that's really frustrating for everyone, including us (1), and I apologize. (3) I want to offer you some alternatives, particularly for those of you who have appointments between three and four o'clock.

First, if you would rather not wait the extra 45 minutes, please come up to the desk and we will reschedule at no charge. If you want to wait because you feel you have to see the doctor today, you don't have to remain in the waiting room. If you want to do something else, just make sure you let me know, and get back here about 35 minutes after your scheduled appointment. That way you won't lose your place. (4)

EXPLANATIONS

Despite what you may think, the most annoying part of having to wait in a waiting room is not the delay or even the lost time, but the uncertainty. The customers are asking themselves, "Should I wait?" "Do I need to call home to arrange child care?" "Can I go and come back?" and similar questions that come from not knowing the situation.

That's the reason why it's absolutely critical to inform waiting customers of the situation. In this example, the receptionist explains the reason for the delay (1). She does this so that the customers know the delay isn't a result of sloppy scheduling or lack of consideration, but due to an unavoidable situation.

She follows this explanation with an empathy statement (2) and an apology. (3) That's basic common courtesy.

Finally she wraps up by providing some alternatives and answering some of the unspoken questions customers probably have. The alternatives, while not perfect, are intended to help the customers make decisions about what they can do to make the delay more tolerable.

HINTS

When making an announcement to a group of people, first ask for their attention. Once you have their attention, then deliver the announcement.

Don't assume that every customer will have heard the group announcement. Some people may not be listening, and it may be necessary to approach each customer individually to explain, just in case he or she didn't hear.

See Also: 2. When a Customer Is in a Hurry, 3. When a Customer Jumps Ahead in a Line of Waiting Customers

58. When a Customer Complains About a Known Problem

THE SITUATION

Sometimes with a product there are problems that employees are aware of, but have not yet been able to correct. The ideal situation is for the employee to inform customers of the problem before the customers have committed to or purchased the problematic item, but that's not always possible. What do you do when a customer complains about a problem that has been identified by employees and/or the company?

TECHNIQUES USED

- Explain Reasoning or Actions (1)
- Apologize (2)
- Bonus Buyoff (3)

DIALOGUE

In this situation, the customer goes to the service desk of a hardware store with a complaint about the bargain gas barbecue he purchased yesterday. His concern is that the product is dented and seems to be missing some parts. This is the third such instance today. The hardware store has determined that the entire shipment is faulty—which it discovered only after selling a number of them.

Customer: I bought this yesterday. There are at least two pieces missing and the top is dented. Why are you selling this junk?

Employee: We only discovered a problem with the shipment this morning, so I apologize for the problem. (1, 2) I'll tell you what I can do to compensate you for the inconvenience. We can exchange this item for the more expensive model, so you'll get more features and quality for the same price. If you have a few minutes, we'll check the more expensive model for you to make sure it's complete. (3) How does that sound?

Customer: Well, OK. That sounds like a good deal.

EXPLANATIONS

Notice that the employee offers a brief explanation of the source of the problem and offers a reason why the customer ended up with a faulty unit (1). The explanation should be brief, because the customer is less interested in the *why* than having a working unit. The employee apologizes for the inconvenience (2), even though he wasn't personally responsible for the problem. He makes his apology on behalf of the company. However, an apology without compensation would be perceived as rather empty.

The employee offers a means of solving the customer's problem by offering two bonus buyoffs (3)—an upgrade to the more expensive model and an offer to inspect the replacement to ensure it is in working order. Pay special attention to the employee's explanation of why the upgrade will be beneficial for the customer.

HINTS

If you do not have the authority to offer a bonus and you are aware of a problem that may affect more than one customer, ask your manager for the authority to deal with this specific problem by offering a bonus. That way, you don't have to involve the manager for each and every instance.

See Also: 55. When You Need to Respond to a Customer Complaint Made in Writing, 56. When a Reservation/Appointment is Lost and You Cannot Meet the Commitment

59. When a Customer Asks Inappropriate Questions

THE SITUATION

You may come across situations where a customer asks questions you deem to be personal and/or not related to the customer service process. These kinds of questions may be quite benign or quite personal and even offensive. How do you handle these situations in a diplomatic and tactful way?

TECHNIQUES USED

- Refocus (1)
- Broken Record (2)

DIALOGUE

During a normal conversation with a customer, the customer starts to ask questions that don't seem to be related to the discussion. Here's how that situation can be addressed.

Customer: So, what's it like to work here?

Employee: I don't want to take up your time talking about my experience here, so perhaps we can get back to discussing the features of the services you are interested in. (1)

Customer: Well, I really want to know what it's like to work here. So what's the scoop?

Employee: It's like any place, really. So, you're interested in our computer repair services? Is there something specific you'd like to know about that? (1, 2)

Customer: Well, I was hoping to apply for a job here and was hoping for a bit more information. But yes, I have a problem with my computer that I need to have fixed.

Employee: I understand. I can't help you with the job, but I can help you with your computer problem. Let's see what we can do. (1, 2)

EXPLANATIONS

While the customer's questions are not that intrusive, the employee does not want to be put in an awkward position by answering them. In this example, the employee layers two techniques, refocus and broken record. Refocusing (1) is intended to encourage the customer to return to the issue that the employee is able and willing to help with. Broken recording (repeating the same theme) is used to reinforce the idea that the employee won't be responding to off-topic questions (2).

HINTS

The broken record technique helps the employee avoid any direct argument and sends a firm but not aggressive message.

The broken record technique works best when you send the same message but in different words. You don't want to repeat the same sentence verbatim. Vary the dialogue.

See Also: 46. When a Customer Wants Information You Are Not Allowed to Give

60. When a Customer Tries an Unacceptable Merchandise Return

THE SITUATION

Most companies have some limits on merchandise returns. Some of those restrictions have to do with safety and/or hygiene reasons (e.g., the return of over-the-counter drugs or undergarments). There is little flexibility possible for accepting returns of such items. Companies may also establish time limits or other conditions regarding returns. For example, they may limit returns to two weeks or allow only exchanges (no refunds) on some items, such as videos and CDs.

Understandably, when you refuse to allow a customer to return an item, it's likely that he or she is going to be upset. Here's a way to handle it.

TECHNIQUES USED

- Probing Questions (1)
- Acknowledging Without Encouraging (2)
- Preemptive Strike (3)
- Providing Alternatives (4)

DIALOGUE

In this situation, the customer is requesting a refund for a boxed set of DVD movies. As is standard, due to the possibility of copying, the store does not accept returns for refunds but only allows an exchange, identical title for title. We join the conversation after the customer has requested his money back.

Employee: I need to ask you one or two questions before we can process this for you. First, were any of the DVDs defective?

Customer: No, they play fine. I just changed my mind.

Employee: Sure, that happens sometimes. (2) When you bought the DVDs from us, did anyone point out our policies on returns and refunds for DVDs? (1)

Customer: I don't remember.

Employee: OK. What I have to tell you isn't going to make you all that happy. (3) Our store and, for that matter, almost all other stores that sell DVDs have an exchange-for-identical-item policy and don't offer refunds. I'd be glad to explain why it's done this way if you'd like, but the bottom line is that we can't refund or exchange it for a different item since the DVD has been opened.

Customer: So you're saying I'm stuck with this?

Employee: Yes, I'm afraid so. As far as I know, we've never made an exception to this rule, but you could talk to the store manager if you'd like. (4)

Customer: No, I can't be bothered. But I'm curious, how was I supposed to know about this "policy," since nobody told me?

Employee: It's so common in the industry that it's possible the cashier forgot to mention it. We also have the policy posted on each rack of DVDs, just in case.

Customer: Well, OK, then.

EXPLANATIONS

In this example, the customer's reactions are relatively mild, and he can best be described as disappointed rather than angry, but that reaction is partly a result of how the employee handled the situation. As soon as the employee learns that none of the DVDs is damaged, he knows the customer isn't going to get what he wants. Rather than simply blurting out "the rule," the employee uses the probing process (1) to build a little bit of rapport with the customer before giving the bad news. He also acknowledges the validity of changing one's mind by acknowledging without encouraging (2). Notice the phrasing, "that happens sometimes," which doesn't agree or disagree with the possibility of a change of mind. The employee does *not* want to make the customer feel stupid and is trying to allow some face-saving here.

In saying, "What I have to tell you isn't going to make you all that happy," the employee uses a preemptive strike (3). Anticipating that the customer may be disappointed, he is the first to identify that the customer is likely to be unhappy with the result. When you acknowledge a customer's emotions in advance, he or she is less likely to harp on those emotions.

In offering the customer an alternative (4), speaking to the manager, the employee is mostly making a gesture of goodwill to placate the customer and show that he is taking the issue seriously, even though he cannot offer the customer what he wants.

Finally, take a close look at how the employee answers the customer's final question about how the store lets people know about the policy. It would be normal to wonder how this customer could not know about this policy that is common in almost every retail store on the planet, could have missed the signs prominently displayed, and could claim he wasn't informed. A less professional employee might have commented in a way that the customer might find offensive or, worse, in a way that might encourage the customer to argue. But this one didn't. He answered the question asked of him and tried to do so without blaming the customer. Why? Because the surest way to generate an argument and waste large amounts of time is to point a blaming finger at a customer, even if it's deserved.

HINTS

When refusing a customer request, it's always good to make some sort of goodwill gesture to the customer along with the refusal. That's not always possible, but if you can, it smoothes the waters. A goodwill gesture would be something that gives the customer "a little something," although not what he wants.

Blaming a customer is plain stupid, even if the customer is to blame. Blame is about embarrassment and humiliation, and people fight back. However, it is appropriate to identify what might have caused a problem, for the purposes of fixing it, which is an unemotional process of gathering information.

See Also: 7. When You Need to Explain a Company Policy or Procedure, 12. When a Customer Needs to Follow a Sequence of Actions